GU01034781

A season of sundays

*Images of the 2022 Gaelic Games year by the Sportsfile team
of photographers, with text by Alan Milton*

An official GAA publication, published by Sportsfile

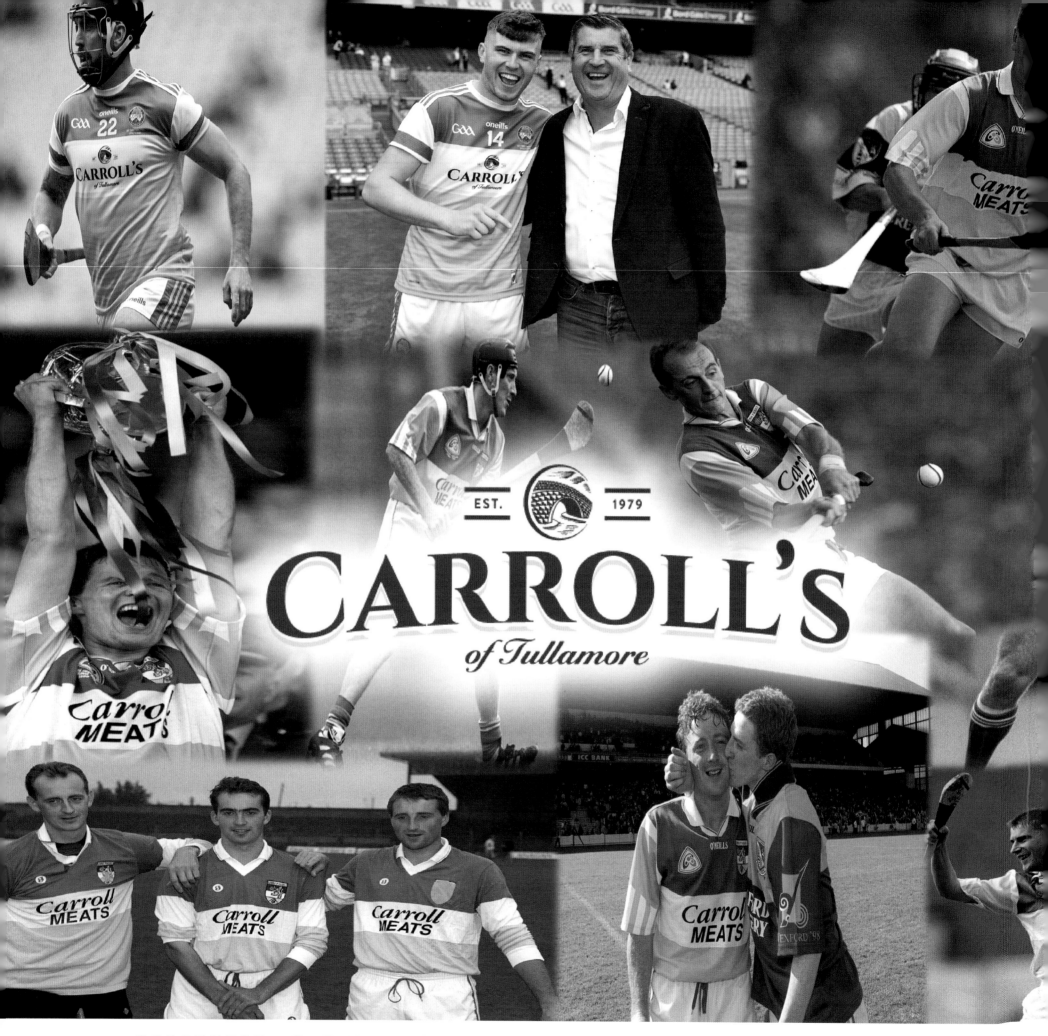

EST. 1979

CARROLL'S
of Tullamore

WWW.CARROLLSOFTULLAMORE.IE

Split season ends on a high note

The much-anticipated 2022 season saw a welcome return to normality – or something very close to normality – in the GAA's intercounty competitions. We were back to full stadiums and sell-out crowds as communities came together in their county colours, a magnificent sight after the disruption caused by Covid in the previous two years.

The format and timetable for the intercounty championships were tweaked this year to give the clubs more time and a bigger profile. As a result of this split season, the All-Ireland hurling final was played on July 17th and the football decider a week later – a huge change from the traditional September dates.

The two big finals were epic spectacles and fitting finales to the season. The supremely athletic Limerick team won the Liam MacCarthy Cup for the third year in a row after a mighty battle against Kilkenny and then Kerry ended their mini-drought by lifting the Sam Maguire Cup for the first time since 2014, again after being pushed all the way by a resurgent Galway.

The ladies football senior title went to Meath for the second year in succession and Kilkenny won the camogie final to round off a wonderful season with credit going to the amazing teams, clubs, and communities all over the country.

We are humbled with the continued support from our local community in Tullamore and, of course, our customers nationwide. When choosing Carroll's of Tullamore, not only will you enjoy the benefits of over 40 years of crafting excellence but you will also be contributing to a proud Irish brand, as we continue to take our time slow-cooking all our meats to perfection, producing delicious ham, award-winning poultry and succulent beef.

Finally, it is with a heavy heart that we mark the end of our 30-year sponsorship of Offaly GAA. Dating back to 1991, Carroll's is recognised as one of the longest-running jersey sponsorships in the association. It has been a great source of pride to support and share in the successes as well as the challenges faced by the Faithful County and we were delighted to see the minor hurlers do so well this year, reaching the All-Ireland final but losing by just a point to Tipperary after giving a terrific display.

We extend our very best wishes to Offaly GAA, all its clubs, players and its loyal and faithful supporters for the future.

– THE CARROLL'S OF TULLAMORE TEAM

sportsfile
PUBLISHING

GAA
OFFICIAL PHOTOGRAPHER

Published by:
SPORTSFILE
Patterson House, 14 South Circular Road
Portobello, Dublin 8, D08 T3FK, Ireland
www.sportsfile.com

Photographs:
Copyright © 2022 Sportsfile

Without limiting the rights under copyright, this book is sold subject to the condition that it shall not, by way of trade or otherwise, be lent, resold, hired out, reproduced, stored in or introduced into a retrieval system, or transmitted, in any form or by any means (electronic, mechanical, photocopying, recording or otherwise), or otherwise circulated, without the publisher's prior consent, in any form other than that in which it is published and without a similar condition, including this condition, being imposed on the subsequent publisher.

ISBN: 978-1-905468-56-0

Text:
Alan Milton

Editing:
Eddie Longworth

Quotations research:
Seán Creedon

Design:
The Design Gang, Tralee

Colour reproduction:
Mark McGrath

Printing / Binding production:
PB Print Solutions

The Sportsfile photographic team:

Ben McShane

Brendan Moran

Dáire Brennan

David Fitzgerald

Diarmuid Greene

Eóin Noonan

Harry Murphy

Matt Browne

Michael P Ryan

Oliver McVeigh

Philip Fitzpatrick

Piaras Ó Mídheach

Ramsey Cardy

Ray McManus

Ray Ryan

Sam Barnes

Seb Daly

Stephen McCarthy

The ice creams are on me – just like the old days

"Get the last of the Lucan Dairy ices – who needs choc ices". That catchcry or sales pitch was a familiar sound at GAA matches to people of a certain generation but, alas, it's one of the many things we don't hear or see anymore.

How times have changed, even since *A Season of Sundays* started back in 1997 with just five photographers. Today we have 18 photographers and thousands of players contributing to this year's edition.

A lot has changed over those 26 years. There are no hawkers selling the ice cream. Nobody jumps the wall. The man or woman with the magic bottle is now a chartered physiotherapist. Full backs are now centre forwards and goalkeepers are everywhere, until they realise they left the immersion on.

And the Lucan Dairy ice cream man is a thing of the past. So, to a large extent, is the hawker scrambling through the supporters with the massive big basket shouting "apples, oranges, bananas or chocolate".

In the old days photographers seldom got good action pictures of the backs as their job was to shift the ball out of their area and let the next man or woman sort things from there. Now it is almost impossible to miss a full back or centre back as they are all in the scoring zone.

All has changed. It is early August and the intercounty season is over for another year. And *A Season of Sundays* is available from October.

But then some things never change. The support of Carroll's of Tullamore continues and ultimately ensures that this book continues to be published. The support of Alan Milton with his ingenious captions, the special assistance of the editor Eddie Longworth and indeed the quotation research by my good friend Seán Creedon are also invaluable.

The book would not be produced without the assistance of the Sportsfile staff, who all contribute in their own way, nor without the long-suffering Minister for Home Affairs – Anne.

The ice creams are on me – some things never change!

Return of full-capacity crowds and more time for clubs are major pluses

Táim breá sásta an deis seo a bheith agam fáilte a chur roimh an bhfoilseachán iontach seo agus ceiliúradh á dhéanamh againn ar bhliain thaitneamhach eile i saol ár gCumainn.

Every GAA season is different but some are more different than others – and 2022 will be remembered by match-goers and supporters for many reasons, not least the return of full-capacity crowds to our games.

As an organisation we were proud of the flexibility and resilience shown by everyone to stage games and competitions during the pandemic but the one thing beyond our organisational capability was the gift of having full houses for our games – and at times any supporters at all.

The staging of All-Ireland finals and indeed many other fixtures at all levels of the organisation, without supporters present, is something we hope we will never have to countenance again

If ever the importance of the connection between those playing on the field and those in the stands and on the terraces was laid bare, it was the empty stadiums of the Covid experience and, thankfully, this was remedied with the commencement of this year's games.

2022 will also be recalled as the year we first trialled a new county/club season outside the pandemic, to provide certainty and space for our clubs. Its success will become evident in the fullness of time.

On the field of play our games, as ever, were memorable on many fronts. Kilcoo and Ballygunner provided All-Ireland club final finishes that outstripped fairy-tale status in claiming national honours for the first time in the most dramatic of circumstances in back-to-back games at Croke Park. Their last-gasp successes encapsulated the joy experienced by Kilmeena and Steelstown (junior and intermediate football) and Mooncoin and Naas (junior and intermediate hurling).

When the Waterford hurlers annexed league honours following the promise shown in recent seasons, hurling's chasing pack seemed well primed to tackle Limerick's three-in-a-row ambitions. Kerry's league football final display underlined the potential of their maturing panel under the guidance of the returning Jack O'Connor.

Our provincial championships threw up the usual supply of drama with Derry's football triumph in Ulster and a truly memorable Munster hurling final two of the stand-out days.

In the middle of it all the Tailteann Cup was unveiled and enthusiastically embraced by the competing counties – none more so than Westmeath who by beating Cavan in Croke Park etched their name in GAA history.

Thereafter, who could forget the penalty shootout drama when Galway beat Armagh, Seán O'Shea's incredible long-range dead-ball winner against Dublin, Gearóid Hegarty's tour de force in Limerick's successful bid for a third successive title or Brian Cody's last act as one of the truly great managers?

We all have takeaway moments and memories of our own. Sometimes it might involve stumbling across a memorable encounter far away from the glare of a Croke Park final or an act of sportsmanship or respect played out away from the masses.

Or the GAA community coming together to mourn the loss of revered players and members such as Tyrone hurler Damian Casey, Galway camogie player Kate Moran or Tipperary hurler Dillon Quirke.

Perhaps it was the community welcome so many of our clubs provided to people displaced by the war in Ukraine.

Many of the shared moments are captured between these two covers because Ray McManus or one of his team of Sportsfile photographers were in attendance and on the look-out.

From the first weeks of our fledgling season until the last trophies are presented, Sportsfile have a presence at countless fixtures and other GAA activities.

Ray's unstinting passion and commitment to this project means *A Season of Sundays* will be available for the 26th consecutive year chronicling our games in a way that may not be fully appreciated until sometime in the future.

Of similar consistency is the support shown by Carroll's to the project, not just this year but for the last 20. Their unwavering support of Gaelic games and projects such as this underlines their commitment to the GAA, and it is greatly appreciated.

All-Ireland finals in July were a new departure but they give our club players the time and the space they deserve as they generate their own levels of excitement through the club championships with no shortage of games across the GAA network.

When it all ends and we pause for a short break we will have this collection of superb images to rejog the memory.

Here's to many more editions.

Beirigí bua.

LARRY MCCARTHY
UACHTARÁN CHUMANN LÚTHCHLEAS GAEL

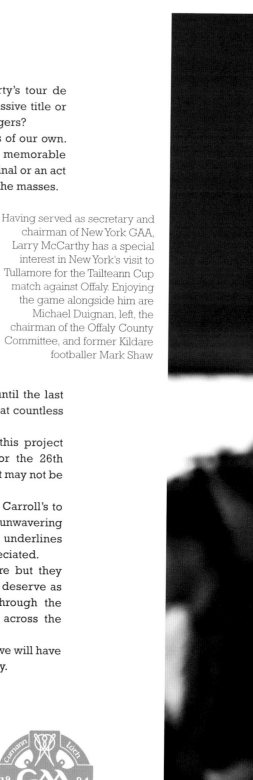

Having served as secretary and chairman of New York GAA, Larry McCarthy has a special interest in New York's visit to Tullamore for the Tailteann Cup match against Offaly. Enjoying the game alongside him are Michael Duignan, left, the chairman of the Offaly County Committee, and former Kildare footballer Mark Shaw

3 Connacht FBD League - NUI Galway Connacht GAA Air Dome, Bekan, Mayo
Sligo 1-21   Leitrim 1-17

5 McGrath Cup - Austin Stack Park, Tralee
Kerry 2-23   Limerick 0-06

2.

(1) A new season. A new beginning. A new voice. And throw in a new venue for good measure – this is the first time a Gaelic football match has been played indoors, specifically in the futuristic Dome in Bekan which can be seen in all its glory overleaf. The new manager is Andy Moran, imparting some of the wisdom and experience he accumulated in a 16-year playing career with Mayo to the Leitrim squad

(2) It's not a completely new beginning for Jack O'Connor, who is starting a third spell in charge of his native Kerry. Having led the Kingdom to three All-Ireland titles (2004, 2006 and 2009) in his earlier terms, another All-Ireland title is the requirement. It's always the requirement in Kerry. His first post-match interview is with Timmy Moynihan of Radio Kerry, with the print journalists awaiting their turn in Austin Stack Park

6 Dr McKenna Cup - Kingspan Breffni, Cavan
Cavan 0-11 Armagh 1-12

7 Connacht FBD League - NUI Galway Connacht GAA Air Dome, Bekan, Mayo
Mayo 0-13 Galway 0-17

1.

2.

(1) Winter postcard. Cavan's outstanding prospect Paddy Lynch – a "serious operator" in Mickey Harte's estimation – shapes to take a free in the opening Dr McKenna Cup fixture, a game that went under the radar at the time but Armagh would make people sit up and take notice as the year unfolds

(2) Build it and they will come. A modern-day Taj Mahal of the west, the Connacht GAA Air Dome captures the imagination of the GAA world in the opening weeks of the year. It is a spectacular sight from on high

7   Dr McKenna Cup - MacCumhaill Park, Ballybofey
Donegal 1-13   Down 2-08

8   O'Byrne Cup - O'Connor Park, Tullamore
Offaly 0-13   Dublin 2-12

(1) It can be cool at McCumhaill. Insulation and hot beverages are the order of the evening as supporters queue for a warming cup of coffee in Ballybofey before venturing out for the clash between Donegal and Down

(2) Another new beginning. Kerry legend Tomás Ó Sé, taking his first steps in intercounty coaching, arrives in O'Connor Park having been appointed to the Offaly backroom team where he will assist manager John Maughan

1.

2.

8 McGrath Cup - Hennessy Memorial Park, Miltown Malbay, Clare
Clare 0-10   Cork 2-09

O'Byrne Cup - Rathcline GAA Club, Lanesboro, Longford
Longford 2-13   Louth 0-14

1.

2.

(1) Every dog has its day. Warming the "subs" bench and no doubt ready to join the fray at a moment's notice, this dog has his eye on the ball at Miltown Malbay

(2) Lanesboro landscaping. The Rathcline club have put their best foot forward for the O'Byrne Cup, which the Longford squad can appreciate as they pose for Syl Healy of the *Longford Leader* and freelance photographer Gerry Rowley

1.

2.

" It's great, but it will count for nothing if we lose our first couple of league games later on "

Hurling manager Stephen Molumphy's reaction is very pragmatic and Kerry-like, despite being a Déise man, when told that his side's win over Tipperary is a first for the county

(1) Laois players should be used to the Kerry accent at this stage as – remarkably – Billy Sheehan is the sixth man from the Kingdom to try to transform the Midlanders' fortunes in recent times. Sheehan may have an advantage on his Kerry predecessors in the hot seat (Mick O'Dwyer, Liam Kearns, Tomás Ó Flatharta, John Sugrue and Mike Quirke) as he enjoyed a fine career in the Laois colours

(2) Straws in the wind. The Kerry senior hurlers record their first win over Tipperary. Ever. It's a sign of the steady progress being made by the Kingdom under new manager Stephen Molumphy and an early portent of a difficult season for the Premier County and their new boss Colm Bonnar. Here, Fionan Mackessy gets the handpass away before Ger Browne can intervene

(3) Staging post number two. Kilmacud Crokes' captain Shane Cunningham lifts the Seán McCabe Cup after his team's Leinster final win over Naas. It brings the south Dublin club's total of provincial titles to five

(4) Out in front. Dublin's Aidan Mellett holds on to the sliotar despite being pressurised by Aaron Crawford of Antrim

4.

9 Walsh Cup - Duggan Park, Ballinasloe
Galway 2-19   Offaly 0-19

AIB Connacht GAA Football Senior Club Championship Final - James Stephens Park, Ballina
Pádraig Pearses 1-13   Knockmore 1-11

(1) They got their man. Expectations are huge in Galway following the appointment of one of the greatest players of all time, Henry Shefflin, as manager. And even if Croke Park on the big occasion is the ultimate destination, starting out in the unglamorous surroundings of Duggan Park will keep him grounded

(2) At last. James Molloy's final whistle is the signal for Pádraig Pearses' joint-captain Emmett Kelly to breathe easily and savour his team's first Connacht club title after a tense finale against Knockmore

1.

2.

9   Walsh Cup - Kelly Daly Park, Rathdowney, Laois
Laois 1-16   Wexford 1-27

AIB Munster Hurling Senior Club Championship Final - Páirc Uí Chaoimh, Cork
Ballygunner 3-20   Kilmallock 1-12

2.

(1) How to make a young fan's day. Nine-year-old Jerry Connors from Gorey, gets a match sliotar from Wexford goalkeeper Mark Fanning, waylaid while gathering up the tools of his trade

(2) They're coming. Eight Waterford championship titles in a row (2015 to 2021) doesn't automatically translate into dominance at national level, and that's the next challenge for Ballygunner. However, after this impressive provincial final win over Kilmallock their delighted players can plan and prepare

12 O'Byrne Cup- Stradbally GAA Club, Laois
Laois 1-12   Meath 0-09

McGrath Cup - Moyne-Templetuohy GAA Club, Tipperary
Tipperary 0-05   Kerry 1-23

2.

(1-2) Park in the dark. The electronic scoreboard at the go-ahead Stradbally club in Laois provides the only light in the car park while 35 miles or so down the road in Templetuohy, steward Paul Kelly helps the Kerry and Tipperary players park in an orderly fashion before the game

(1) Crutches down, ladders up. It's a case of getting up and dirty for Ciarán Barnes and Gary Prunty while erecting the scoreboard at the Bray Emmets club before proceedings get under way

(2) Things are looking up. Brian Fenton and these two young Dublin supporters are all smiles facing the camera after a routine victory over Louth

(3) Leaning under the half door. Galway goalkeeper Conor Flaherty ducks under the automated door as he and his team-mates return to the Dome pitch after half-time and retain the Connacht League

1.

12 O'Byrne Cup - Bray Emmets GAA Club, Wicklow
Wicklow 1-11   Wexford 1-07

O'Byrne Cup - Parnell Park, Dublin
Dublin 3-19   Louth 1-10

14 Connacht FBD League Final - NUI Galway Connacht GAA Air Dome, Bekan, Mayo
Galway 1-18   Roscommon 1-16

2.

3.

15 Dr McKenna Cup - O'Neills Healy Park, Omagh
Tyrone 1-15 Armagh 2-15

O'Byrne Cup - Crettyard GAA Club, Laois
Laois 2-14 Wicklow 1-11

1.

(1) The lure of a magnet, and a reminder that Tyrone are the reigning All-Ireland
champions. Marie McNeillis, Frances Storey, Noeleen McCann, Martin Grainger
and Mark McCann, all members of the Omagh unit of The Order of Malta, pose
for a photograph with the Sam Maguire Cup at Healy Park

(2) The Special Branch. A steward has many duties and skills including being
a tree climber, and here Pat Reilly battles with nature in an effort to retrieve
a stray football in Crettyard. At €50 a pop, it's worth the effort

2.

15 O'Byrne Cup - Donaghmore Ashbourne GAA Club, Meath
Meath 1-15   Wexford 1-10

16 Walsh Cup - John Lockes GAA Club, Callan, Kilkenny
Kilkenny 1-27   Laois 0-24

AIB Ulster GAA Football Senior Club Championship Final - Athletic Grounds, Armagh
Kilcoo Owen Roes 3-10   Derrygonnelly Harps 0-03

1.

2.

3.

(1) Sometimes sport comes a distant second. The murder of 23-year-old schoolteacher Ashling Murphy while walking along the Grand Canal in Tullamore touches the nation and the wider GAA family rally around. The Wexford footballers pay their respects to Ashling, a keen camogie player with the Kilcormac-Killoughey club, with a floral tribute and a simple, heartfelt message after their match in Ashbourne

(2) The barriers are up but Lockes is open. The chairman of the John Lockes club in Callan, Seán Hogan, left, and Jimmy Corcoran attend to one of the many chores involved in hosting a match

(3) Surveying the situation. John-Joe Branagan, son of Kilcoo joint-captain Aidan Branagan, peers over the Séamus McFerran Cup after his team secure a second Ulster club title, backing up their breakthrough success in 2019

1.

2.

16 AIB Munster GAA Football Senior Club Championship Final - Semple Stadium, Thurles
St Finbarr's 2-09   Austin Stacks 1-10

Walsh Cup - Parnell Park, Dublin
Dublin 3-29   Galway 0-19

19 O'Byrne Cup - Netwatch Cullen Park, Carlow
Laois 1-06   Kildare 0-09   (Laois win 6-5 on penalties)

3.

(1) Not this time. A disappointed Conor Jordan of Austin Stacks ponders the Kerry team's narrow defeat in the Munster club final to St Finbarr's, who win their fifth title (now the Michael O'Connor Cup) and first since 1986

(2) Screw-ins or mouldies. Galway manager Henry Shefflin gives the pitch a thorough inspection before the game, perhaps aware that Parnell Park is generally not a happy hunting ground for the Tribesmen. The final score bears out those fears, with Dublin marksman Donal Burke leading the destruction with an 18-point haul

(3) Toeing the line. A penalty shootout under floodlights may not be a goalkeeper's idea of fun but Laois's Matthew Byron is up to the task, making the decisive save against Kildare. Penalty shootouts will increase in regularity with 'finish on the day' adopted for a greater number of games

22 McGrath Cup Final - Fitzgerald Stadium, Killarney
Kerry 2-17   Cork 0-11

O'Byrne Cup Final - Netwatch Cullen Park, Carlow
Dublin 1-13   Laois 0-11

Walsh Cup - Chadwicks Wexford Park, Wexford
Wexford 2-25   Kilkenny 2-25

1.

(1) Going the extra mile. Kerry supporter Michael D Mahony makes his case for David Clifford's jersey and extends birthday wishes on a day when Kerry claim McGrath Cup honours against Cork. Ten out of ten to the 10-year-old for initiative

(2) It could only be Carlow. The county's distinctive colours provide the backdrop as Dublin captain Ciarán Kilkenny makes his way down the tunnel in Dr Cullen Park with the O'Byrne Cup trophy

(3) Neck and neck. Kilkenny's Colm Prenderville is not for stopping as Simon Donohoe of Wexford attempts to apply the brakes

JANUARY '22

23 Co-op Superstores Munster Hurling Cup Final - Cusack Park, Ennis
Clare 0-18 Limerick 0-27

AIB GAA Hurling All-Ireland Senior Club Championship Semi-Final - FBD Semple Stadium, Thurles
Shamrocks Ballyhale 2-15 St Thomas' 0-20

1.

(1) The umpire pushes back. Referee Conor Doyle holds his own in the wrestling session that precedes many a hurling throw-in, this time involving Clare's Paddy Donnellan, left, and Jack Browne, right, and the Limerick duo Brian O'Grady and Will O'Donoghue. It's Limerick's first silverware of the season and the first of four clashes between the teams in 2022

(2) "Luckily enough I put my hurley in a bucket of water last night just to give the bás a bit more weight… I got it on the sweet spot. I couldn't have struck it any better." TJ Reid wheels away after striking a last-minute free to the net and breaking St Thomas' hearts. The Galway side did nothing wrong in this match, they had one foot in the All-Ireland club final but were undone by the most famous bucket in Ballyhale

" I asked the ref what was left and he said 30 seconds so I had only one option and that was to go for goal. It was pure luck that it went in **"**

TJ Reid is typically modest about his late dramatic free that gave Ballyhale Shamrocks a one-point win over St Thomas' of Galway in the All-Ireland club hurling semi-final

29 AIB GAA Football All-Ireland Senior Club Championship Semi-Final - Kingspan Breffni, Cavan
Kilmacud Crokes 1-11   Pádraig Pearses 0-08

AIB GAA Football All-Ireland Senior Club Championship Semi-Final - MW Hire O'Moore Park, Portlaoise
Kilcoo Owen Roes 1-18   St Finbarr's 1-13

Walsh Cup Final - Croke Park, Dublin
Dublin 2-29   Wexford 0-19

Allianz Football League - Croke Park, Dublin
Dublin 1-13   Armagh 2-15

1.

2.

3.

" There is definitely a significant amount of transition going on. A lot of core players have left the squad over the last two to three years and we are trying to replace that quality **"**

Dublin football manager Dessie Farrell after their opening-day league defeat to Armagh at Croke Park

(1) Smokescreen. Lorcán Daly of Pádraig Pearses battles against Craig Dias and the conditions in Cavan, with Kilmacud Crokes advancing to their third All-Ireland club final

(2) Digesting it all. Alan O'Connor of St Finbarr's processes the disappointment of losing a semi-final in extra-time but Kilcoo are on target to go all the way after their extra-time defeat to Corofin in the 2020 final

(3) Eoghan O'Donnell gets a hug from his mother Mary after Dublin win the Walsh Cup final. That's the same Eoghan O'Donnell who is called up to the Dublin football panel later in the season

(4) The Football League begins with a bang. Armagh manager Kieran McGeeney delivers his message with gusto after his newly-promoted side stun Dublin in Croke Park with Rian O'Neill turning on the style in a team performance that raises eyebrows

4.

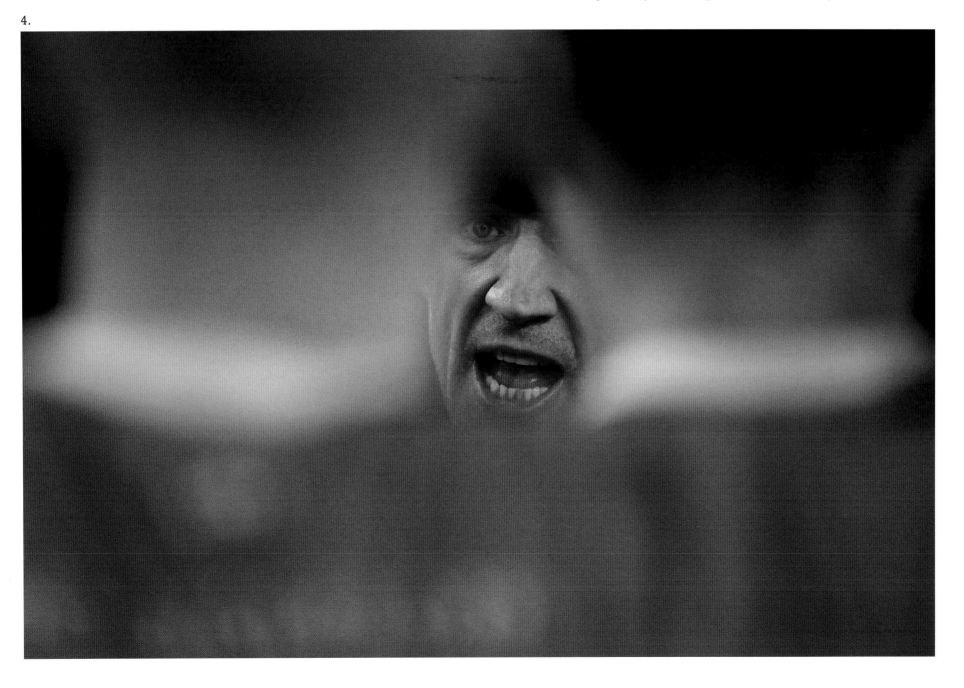

30 Allianz Football League - Dr Hyde Park, Roscommon
Roscommon 1-13 Cork 0-10

Allianz Football League - St Conleth's Park, Newbridge
Kildare 0-13 Kerry 1-10

Allianz Football League - Pearse Stadium, Salthill
Galway 1-14 Meath 0-06

Allianz Football League - Chadwicks Wexford Park, Wexford
Wexford 0-10 Sligo 0-12

Allianz Football League - Markievicz Park, Sligo
Mayo 0-11 Donegal 0-11

Allianz Football League - O'Neills Healy Park, Omagh
Tyrone 0-09 Monaghan 0-09

2.

1.

3.

4.

(1) Hiding at the Hyde. A downpour is the guaranteed way of clearing the terraces of supporters and officials in the winter months

(2) That fixtures computer. In the first league game of his third stint as Kerry manager, Jack O'Connor is sent back to Newbridge to face Kildare, the team he managed the previous two seasons. The implications of an early return to his (not too) old stomping ground aren't lost on O'Connor: "This was always going to be a tricky game for me… I gave it absolutely everything when I was up here"

(3) The umpire signalling another Galway point just underlines Meath's inability to give him much to do. The Royals don't score until the 45th minute, by which stage they are 1-11 to 0-0 down – at least they don't wave the white flag

(4) A chip off the old block. Pat Spillane junior, who joined Sligo this year under the parentage rule as his mother Rosarii hails from the Yeats County, is congratulated by his manager Tony McEntee

(5) Donegal defender Brendan McCole loses his footing under pressure from Mayo's Ryan O'Donoghue

(6) Getting the quotes. Besides writing a match report, a reporter must also record the views of the managers, and that often means hanging around long after the game is over. At Healy Park, Monaghan manager Séamus McEnaney is his usual obliging self as he talks to RTÉ's Pauric Lodge, left, and the doyen of GAA reporters, Seán Moran of *The Irish Times*

5.

6.

5

Allianz Football League - Austin Stack Park, Tralee
Kerry 1-15   Dublin 0-11

Allianz Hurling League - MW Hire O'Moore Park, Portlaoise
Laois 1-14   Tipperary 0-21

Allianz Hurling League - Páirc Uí Chaoimh, Cork
Cork 2-30   Clare 2-21

1.

3.

(1) It's a young person's game these days. The youthful faces outnumber the more seasoned features in the stand before the start but the Kerry-Dublin rivalry appeals to all generations, even if this match is untypically one-sided

(2) In the zone. Tipperary manager Colm Bonnar, notes in hand and with his game face on, stands in the visiting dressing-room in O'Moore Park before the match. Bonnar has a tough act to follow after the departure of Liam Sheedy and the retirement of some senior players, and with an urgent rebuilding job top of his agenda

(3) Shortening the grip because the hook is coming. Clare's Ryan Taylor, thriving under manager Brian Lohan, attempts to get his shot away as Cork corner back Niall O'Leary goes full stretch

6   Allianz Football League - Athletic Grounds, Armagh
Armagh 2-14   Tyrone 0-14

11   AIB GAA Hurling All-Ireland Senior Club Championship Final - Croke Park, Dublin
Ballygunner 2-17   Shamrocks Ballyhale 1-19

1.

" I've never seen anything like that in my life and I've been around a lot of football "

Tyrone joint-manager Feargal Logan's reaction to five players being dismissed in one go

(1)   Zero tolerance approach. Referee David Gough isn't putting up with any nonsense following a melee at the end of this game and takes the radical step of ordering off four Tyrone players at the same time – from left, Kieran McGeary, Peter Harte, Michael McKernan and Pádraig Hampsey. That's five players off and 12 yellow cards doled out

(2)   Hotspot. Pitch lamps, used to encourage grass growth, heat the Davin End goalmouth in Croke Park the night before the All-Ireland club hurling and football finals

2.

12   AIB GAA Hurling All-Ireland Senior Club Championship Final - Croke Park, Dublin
Ballygunner 2-17   Shamrocks Ballyhale 1-19

AIB GAA Football All-Ireland Senior Club Championship Final - Croke Park, Dublin
Kilcoo Owen Roes 2-08   Kilmacud Crokes 0-13

1.

Mirror Images I...

Sometimes sport throws up games that unfold in a remarkably similar way. This year's senior club finals are a case in point with two exhilarating contests, last-gasp decisive goals, come-from-behind victories, novel winners and scenes of unbridled joy

(1-3) A shot by Ballygunner's Harry Ruddle (not in picture) evades the hurley of Ballyhale goalkeeper Dean Mason to snatch victory at the death in an unforgettable finish to the club hurling final; a young Ballygunner supporter celebrates his team's success; an emotional Harry Ruddle, left, gets a hug from team-mate Barry Coughlan

2.

3.

4.

5.

6.

(4-6) Not to be outdone, the football final also produces a thrilling finale as Jerome Johnston scores Kilcoo's second goal, in extra-time; Dylan Ward, left, and Anthony Morgan of Kilcoo celebrate the late snatch-and-grab raid that left Kilmacud shell-shocked; a jubilant Kilcoo supporter rejoices after a result that few saw coming

12 AIB GAA Hurling All-Ireland Senior Club Championship Final - Croke Park, Dublin
Ballygunner 2-17   Shamrocks Ballyhale 1-19

AIB GAA Football All-Ireland Senior Club Championship Final - Croke Park, Dublin
Kilcoo Owen Roes 2-08   Kilmacud Crokes 0-13

1.

2.

3.

Mirror Images II...

(1-3) It's said that the moments after the final whistle are the best and Paddy Leavey's reaction to Ballygunner's victory backs this up; Philip O'Mahony, left, and Barry Coughlan raise the Tommy Moore Cup; the Ballygunner panel and management team pose for a celebratory photo after reaching the pinnacle of the club game

4.

5.

6.

(4-6) In an emotional gesture, Kilcoo joint captains Conor Laverty, left, and Aidan Branagan would not accept the trophy until they were joined by team manager Mickey Moran; Jerome Johnston celebrates with his five-month-old son Lar; the Kilcoo squad, backroom team and even some youngsters gather with the Andy Merrigan Cup

❝ He doesn't want the limelight, he doesn't want people talking about him. Mickey doesn't want to be the story ❞

Kilcoo's Conleth Gilligan pays tribute to fellow manager Mickey Moran

12 Allianz Hurling League - Corrigan Park, Belfast
Antrim 2-15   Dublin 2-19

Allianz Hurling League - TUS Gaelic Grounds, Limerick
Limerick 1-18   Galway 0-27

13 Allianz Hurling League - FBD Semple Stadium, Thurles
Tipperary 1-19   Kilkenny 1-18

Allianz Hurling League - Walsh Park, Waterford
Waterford 7-31   Laois 0-19

19 Allianz Football League - Athletic Grounds, Armagh
Armagh 1-07   Monaghan 0-10

2.

1.

3.

4.

(1-3) Hectic and helter-skelter. The swirling movement and wild patterns of
the greatest field game in the world are captured in these images: Dublin's
Rian McBride tries to put distance between himself and a posse led by Eoghan
Campbell of Antrim; Galway's Pádraic Mannion is subjected to a five-man press
by Limerick; and Kilkenny's Huw Lawlor contests an aerial battle with
the Tipperary trio of, from left, Denis Maher, Ger Browne and Mark Kehoe

(4) No need to read the match report. This sort of scoreline is always a possibility
when a team crippled by injuries – as Laois were – meet a top-tier county with
big ambitions. Of more significance for Waterford is the return of Tadhg de Burca,
making his first start since the 2020 All-Ireland final when he suffered the second
cruciate knee injury of his career

(5) Exit route. Armagh's Jarly Óg Burns finds an unconventional way out of this
scrum-maul despite the squeeze applied by Monaghan players, from left, Ryan
Wylie, Darren Hughes and Conor Boyle

5.

19   Allianz Football League - Croke Park, Dublin
      Dublin 0-12   Mayo 2-11

20   Allianz Football League - Páirc Tailteann, Navan
      Meath 2-06   Down 2-06

(1) Rory Brickenden of Mayo blocks a shot by Lee Gannon but there's no blocking the rise of the stylish young Dublin player who is nailing down a place on Dessie Farrell's team with a string of consistent performances

(2) Ground control to the halfway line. There's a cruel irony in suspended Meath boss Andy McEntee, right, having to sit in an event controller's box – the very place from where a manager has least control over a game. At least he's keeping out of trouble

1.

2.

EVENT CONTROLLER

20 Allianz Football League - Connacht GAA Centre of Excellence, Bekan, Mayo
Leitrim 0-09   London 2-05

Allianz Football League - Fitzgerald Stadium, Killarney
Kerry 1-13   Donegal 0-07

Allianz Football League - O'Neills Healy Park, Omagh
Tyrone 2-07   Kildare 0-12

1.

3.

(1) Shattering the glass ceiling. Maggie Farrelly makes GAA history by becoming the first woman to referee a men's National Football League game. The Cavan woman said afterwards: "Just because you're a lady doesn't mean you are going to get different treatment (from the men) – you definitely don't," although Leitrim veteran Emlyn Mulligan is showing respect

(2) The project proceeds apace. Jack O'Connor celebrates a late score as his Kerry team maintain their push for league honours

(3) A roller-coaster race. The Healy Park groundsmen earned their crust before this game – in fact, they performed a near miracle in getting the pitch ready for the visit of Kildare given the horrendous conditions that Sunday with several games called off because of Storm Franklin

" It's not a huge priority to win the league. If we can experiment a bit and win a few matches that's basically it. But winning matches does give confidence to a group of players **"**

Kerry football manager Jack O'Connor plays down ambitions to win the National League following a big victory over Donegal

26 Allianz Football League - MacCumhaill Park, Ballybofey
Donegal 2-10   Tyrone 0-12

Allianz Hurling League - FBD Semple Stadium, Thurles
Tipperary 0-21   Dublin 2-16

Allianz Football League - O'Connor Park, Tullamore
Offaly 1-10   Meath 1-10

Allianz Football League - Páirc Uí Chaoimh, Cork
Cork 2-17   Galway 3-22

27 Allianz Football League - Dr Hyde Park, Roscommon
Mayo 0-15   Armagh 1-10

1.

2.

3.

4.

❝ I feel like Job at the moment. Everything that can go wrong is going wrong ❞

A rueful Cork football manager Keith Ricken following a heavy – but not quite biblical – defeat to Galway at Páirc Uí Chaoimh

5.

(1) The difficult second record. Tyrone joint-manager Brian Dooher, with goalkeeper Niall Morgan in the background, has worries aplenty as the challenges defending champions face become apparent

(2) So close. Jason Forde's attempt on goal in the final seconds comes to nought and Dublin withstand the Tipperary comeback with just a point to spare

(3) Tied up in the tackle and tied at the final whistle. Meath's Eoin Harkin is bottled up by Jack Bryant, right, and Colm Doyle of Offaly in a Division Two match that feels like a relegation battle even at this early stage

(4) It's not often you score 2-17 in a football match and lose. With Cork also sucked into the Division Two relegation battle, their manager Keith Ricken has a word afterwards with Ian Maguire, who fortunately wasn't marking the unstoppable Shane Walsh who struck 2-7 of Galway's total

(5) The star attraction even after the game. Not many supporters normally bother to stay for the warm-down but the Mayo fan club is as enthusiastic as ever and Aidan O'Shea is the centre of attention in Hyde Park

27 Allianz Hurling League - TUS Gaelic Grounds, Limerick
Limerick 1-13   Cork 2-19

Allianz Hurling League - Pearse Stadium, Salthill
Galway 0-15   Wexford 2-15

Allianz Football League - Páirc Grattan, Inniskeen, Monaghan
Monaghan 1-12   Kerry 3-14

1.

2.

❝ I thought our first half was very good, we were very competitive. We did a lot of good things, but in the second half I thought we were sloppy at times ❞

Cork hurling manager Kieran Kingston assesses a fine nine-point win over Limerick at the Gaelic Grounds

(1) Seldom in the shadows. Limerick manager John Kiely is interviewed before a rare defeat, at home to Cork. Even at this stage of the season – and despite a performance that Kiely describes as "really, really poor" – it isn't hard to think both he and Limerick have bigger fish to fry later in the year

(2 Stranger than fiction. Wexford's Damien Reck tries to slow down Niall Burke of Galway on a day when a Leaving Cert student, 18-year-old Oisín Pepper, scores the decisive second goal and then travels home on the team bus with his teacher in St Mary's CBS in Enniscorthy, Kevin Foley, who was captaining Wexford for the first time

(3) Cash isn't king at cashless matches. Monaghan County Board treasurer Eileen Keenan, left, chats with Marion Donnelly while monitoring matters on a quiet day at the office

27 Allianz Football League - St Conleth's Park, Newbridge
Kildare 1-12   Dublin 0-12

5 Lidl Ladies Football National League Division 1B- Páirc Tailteann, Navan
Meath 1-08   Dublin 1-09

1.

2.

(1) The Dream Team are in dreamland. After a first league or championship win over Dublin for 22 years, it's no wonder Kildare's big-name management team of former players Anthony Rainbow, left, manager Glenn Ryan and Dermot Earley are ecstatic at the final whistle. After four successive defeats, the unthinkable is becoming the mentionable for the Dubs – relegation from Division One

(2) The Dublin-Meath rivalry is as intense as ever, but these days it's the women who are pulling in the crowds and providing the epic encounters. Meath scooped the jackpot last year beating their rivals in the All-Ireland final but Dublin edge this league clash

2.

3.

4.

(1) Head turner. There's no lapse in concentration or attention among this group of spectators who are focused totally on the play towards the Killester End in Parnell Park

(2) Respect. The Cork players observe a minute's silence for Henry Shefflin's younger brother, Paul, who died suddenly while out running on the Friday before the game. In the sombre evening setting, Cork manager Kieran Kingston captures the mood: "Hurling, and all that goes with it, is way down the list when it comes to situations like this"

(3-4) Blue skies, long shadows. Niall Daly of Galway warms up before the game while the Clare players assemble for the traditional team photograph. It won't be the first time this year that there's nothing between Clare and Limerick after 70 minutes' play

1.

2.

12 Allianz Football League - Athletic Grounds, Armagh
Armagh 1-12   Kildare 0-10

Allianz Football League - Austin Stack Park, Tralee
Kerry 1-12   Mayo 0-14

13 Allianz Football League - O'Neills Healy Park, Omagh
Tyrone 0-08   Dublin 0-13

Allianz Football League - MacCumhaill Park, Ballybofey
Donegal 0-10   Monaghan 1-12

4.

(1) They're not doing it for the glamour. Oblivious to the driving rain, Armagh manager Kieran McGeeney patrols the sideline and soaks it all in

(2) Tony Brosnan, whose goal was vital in this Kerry victory, urges on his colleagues after scoring a second-half point

(3) Dean Rock makes things awkward for goalkeeper Niall Morgan just as Dublin make life difficult for Tyrone on their own patch. Dublin thus record their first league win of the season, with all their points coming from play and building a half-time lead of 0-11 to 0-2. Who says Dublin are finished

(4) Donegal supporters cross the Finn River pedestrian walkway with their customary optimism – after all, they haven't seen their team lose a league match in Ballybofey for 12 years. But records are there to be broken, and Monaghan do so with their first league win of the year

19 Allianz Football League - O'Neills Healy Park, Omagh
Tyrone 0-11   Mayo 0-09

20 Allianz Hurling League - TUS Gaelic Grounds, Limerick
Limerick 4-29   Offaly 0-17

Allianz Football League - Athletic Grounds, Armagh
Armagh 0-13   Kerry 1-13

Allianz Hurling League - St Conleth's Park, Newbridge
Kildare 0-14   Westmeath 1-22

1.

2.

3.

4.

(1) Synchronised entry. The Tyrone players bound on to Healy Park with a spring in their step, and why not – they're the reigning All-Ireland champions and champions generally show some swagger, even after a setback

(2) Young hurlers on the ditch. There may be some juvenile coaching going on as these Limerick lads call out to Aaron Gillane before the game

(3) Jack O'Connor mingles with supporters in the stand while waiting for a delayed throw-in at the Athletic Grounds

(4) Johnny Bermingham tries to burst through the tackles of Kildare's Jack Sheridan, left, and Cathal Dowling as Westmeath's hurlers maintain their promotion push under new manager Joe Fortune

20 Allianz Hurling League - FBD Semple Stadium, Thurles
Tipperary 7-28 Antrim 1-17

Allianz Hurling League - Pearse Stadium, Salthill
Galway 0-25 Clare 1-20

Allianz Football League - St Conleth's Park, Newbridge
Kildare 0-24 Monaghan 1-12

Allianz Hurling League - UPMC Nowlan Park, Kilkenny
Kilkenny 2-21 Waterford 0-21

Allianz Football League - Glennon Brothers Pearse Park, Longford
Longford 2-13 Wicklow 0-20

Allianz Football League - FBD Semple Stadium, Thurles
Tipperary 2-16 Carlow 0-11

2.

3.

4.

1.

(1) Tipperary round off their league campaign in some style with one of their younger lads, Conor Stakelum, striking at goal under pressure from Antrim's Keelan Molloy

(2) Retrofit. Aaron Fitzgerald of Clare wins an aerial duel against Galway's Conor Whelan on a day when both counties don old-style jerseys to mark the 30th anniversary of Allianz's sponsorship of the National Hurling and Football Leagues. Allianz first became title sponsor of the leagues in the 1993/94 season

(3) The managers' indecision is final. The Kildare brains trust of selectors Anthony Rainbow, Dermot Earley and Johnny Doyle and manager Glenn Ryan discuss possible half-time changes

(4) Take One. RTÉ Raidió na Gaeltachta's Dáithí de Mórdha, right, awaits his cue to interview Kilkenny players Richie Reid, left, and man of the match David Blanchfield. Covid hasn't gone away

(5) Longford's top scorer on the day, Jack Duggan, tries to block a shot by Patrick O'Keane of Wicklow as the fight to avoid relegation intensifies in Division Three

(6) Home alone. The famous face looking on in an empty stand in Semple Stadium is Declan Browne, one of Tipperary's greatest footballers and now a selector. Only three All Star football awards have gone to Tipp and Browne has two of them, won in 1998 and 2003

5.

6.

1.

2.

" We have appointed a new management team and they have gone for youth. We have been very successful at underage, winning minor and under-20 All-Irelands, so the talent is there. It just takes time to bring it through "

Cork County Board vice-chairman Pat Horgan strikes an optimistic note following the Rebels' victory over Down, their first in the 2022 football league campaign

20 Allianz Football League - Derry GAA Centre of Excellence, Owenbeg
Derry 0-12   Galway 4-11

Allianz Hurling League - Chadwicks Wexford Park, Wexford
Wexford 1-22   Cork 1-17

Allianz Football League - Páirc Uí Chaoimh, Cork
Cork 1-16   Down 1-12

Allianz Football League - Croke Park, Dublin
Dublin 2-15   Donegal 2-11

3.

4.

(1) The players' body language tells the story. Chrissy McKaigue leads a disconsolate bunch of Derry players off the field after their promotion push is derailed by Galway, whom they would meet later in the year in a big championship clash

(2) The next wave. Jack O'Connor is the player signing the various sticks and sliotars presented by Wexford's young hurling fans – no doubt the requests for selfies will follow

Playing the game wasn't as stressful as this business. Two of Ulster's finest players in their day, (3) Down's James McCartan and (4) Donegal's Declan Bonner, are feeling the heat of management amid relegation battles. McCartan's team are already destined for Division Three and he has remarked, perhaps tongue-in-cheek: "The blanket defences are a bit alien to me and I'm having to learn quickly. I prefer the good old days"

1.

2.

3.

26   Allianz Hurling League Semi-Final - Páirc Uí Chaoimh, Cork
Cork 1-27   Kilkenny 2-20

Allianz Hurling League Relegation Play-Off - Páirc Tailteann, Navan
Antrim 2-24   Offaly 2-17

27   Allianz Football League - Fitzgerald Stadium, Killarney
Kerry 2-11   Tyrone 1-15

Allianz Football League - O'Connor Park, Tullamore
Offaly 1-20   Cork 1-21

Allianz Football League - Páirc Tailteann, Navan
Meath 2-11   Derry 1-16

4.

5.

(1) Sensing something in the night air. After reaching their first league final since 2015, Cork supporters suddenly seem more optimistic as they swarm on to Páirc Uí Chaoimh

(2) Letting nothing slip through the net. Umpire Frank Mee ties up a few loose strings in Páirc Tailteann ahead of the game

(3) The men in black are not seeing eye to eye. Tyrone goalkeeper Niall Morgan's protests won't change referee David Coldrick's decision to award a penalty to Kerry

(4) When you're down. Friends and family try to console Anton Sullivan after Offaly narrowly lose a last-day relegation battle with Cork

(5) Eleven league points is usually sufficient to win promotion but, unfortunately for Derry, it's not enough in a competitive Division Two. The visitors' frustration won't overly concern Slane officials John Mongey and Seán Fox who are enjoying the spring rays

27 Allianz Football League - O'Donnell Park, Letterkenny
Donegal 1-14   Armagh 1-13

Allianz Football League - County Grounds, Aughrim
Wicklow 1-13   Louth 2-17

Allianz Football League - St Tiernach's Park, Clones
Monaghan 3-13   Dublin 1-18

Allianz Football League - Avant Money Páirc Seán Mac Diarmada, Carrick-on-Shannon
Mayo 2-20   Kildare 0-18

1.

2.

3.

(1) Let's twist again. Despite the unorthodox body positions, Armagh midfielder Ben Crealey seems to have control of the ball under pressure from Caolan Ward of Donegal

(2) Never lost it. One of the most successful managers in the game, Mickey Harte, takes the acclaim after steering Louth to a second successive promotion in the league

(3) The man who sank Dublin. One of the stories of the year is Dublin's relegation from Division One due in no small part to Jack McCarron whose tally of 2-6 included converting a penalty, lobbing the goalkeeper for a cheeky goal and kicking the winning free five minutes into injury-time. His mother Patricia is one of the first to congratulate him followed by most of Monaghan, the great escape artists

(4) The Tour de Connacht. Pitch work at MacHale Park means Mayo had to take to the road for their home games in the league. Their fans follow – to Markievicz Park, Hyde Park and finally Páirc Seán Mac Diarmada which is kind to them against Kildare

4.

2   Allianz Hurling League Division 3A Final - Derry GAA Centre of Excellence, Owenbeg
    Tyrone 2-21   Armagh 2-19

    Allianz Hurling League Division 3B Final - Avant Money Páirc Seán Mac Diarmada Carrick-on-Shannon
    Fermanagh 2-18   Longford 1-17

    Allianz Hurling League Division 2A Final - FBD Semple Stadium, Thurles
    Westmeath 5-19   Down 1-17

    Allianz Football League Division 4 Final - Croke Park, Dublin
    Cavan 2-10   Tipperary 0-15

    Allianz Football League Division 3 Final - Croke Park, Dublin
    Louth 1-14   Limerick 0-12

(1-5) The winners' enclosure. The end of the leagues is nigh which is cue for one of the busiest weeks in the GAA intercounty calendar for trophy presentation. The hurlers of Tyrone, Fermanagh and Westmeath and the footballers of Cavan and Louth accept the silverware and the plaudits amid wild celebrations at Croke Park

3.

1.

2.

4

2 Allianz Hurling League Division 1 Final - FBD Semple Stadium, Thurles
   Waterford 4-20   Cork 1-23

3 Allianz Football League Division 2 Final - Croke Park, Dublin
   Roscommon 1-20   Galway 0-22

   Lidl Ladies Football National League Division 3 Final - St Brendan's Park, Birr
   Roscommon 0-09   Wexford 1-05

   Allianz Football League Division 1 Final - Croke Park, Dublin
   Kerry 3-19   Mayo 0-13

10 Nicky Rackard Cup - St Mary's GAA Club, Maguiresbridge
   Fermanagh 2-13   Donegal 1-21

2.

1.

3.

4.

(1) Silverware speaks for itself. With Carthach Daly jinking around the combined tackles of Cork's Darragh Fitzgibbon, left, and Ger Millerick, Waterford win their fourth league title and first since 2015 – adding to the feel-good factor in the Déise following Ballygunner's All-Ireland club triumph

(2-3) Double celebration for Roscommon. What the men can do in Croke Park, the women, led by captain Laura Fleming, can do in Birr where Rosie Lennon scored the winning free three minutes from time – a case of Rosie leading the Rossies

(4) Unmarkable. David Clifford lets fly past Mayo goalkeeper Rory Byrne for his team's third goal after rounding his marker, the unlucky Pádraig O'Hora who was left chasing shadows all day. The league title is headed to the Kingdom and it's on to the next phase of the Jack Slam

(5) Donegal personnel Shane Sweeney, Gavin Browne, physiotherapist Neil McAuley, Oisín Marley, Mark Curran, Steven Gillespie, Thomas Hartnett, Paul Nelson, Cathal Doherty and James Hartnett follow the play as the championship begins with the Nicky Rackard Cup competition

5.

10 Lidl Ladies Football National League Division 1 Final - Croke Park, Dublin
Meath 2-08   Donegal 1-09

16 Leinster GAA Hurling Senior Championship - TEG Cusack Park, Mullingar
Westmeath 1-19   Kilkenny 5-23

Ulster GAA Football Senior Championship - Brewster Park, Enniskillen
Fermanagh 2-10   Tyrone 2-17

Leinster GAA Hurling Senior Championship - Parnell Park, Dublin
Dublin 1-20   Laois 2-15

3.

1.

2.

4.

(1) The Meath ladies, just nine months in the senior ranks, prove that their 2021 All-Ireland success was no flash in the pan by adding the league title after a close battle with an emerging Donegal outfit. Manager Eamonn Murray, celebrating with Vikki Wall, jokes afterwards: "There isn't much left to win now – Husband of the Year maybe"

(2) The kitmen's union. Kilkenny kitman Rackard Cody starts his 45th championship in the role over a chat and a cup of tea with his Westmeath counterpart, Keith Quinn. Forty-five years' service – it's a labour of love for one of the GAA's most dedicated volunteers

(3) Screen time. Fermanagh football manager Kieran Donnelly is subject to multiple recordings while giving his thoughts to the media after a creditable performance against Tyrone. Smartphones and other technological advances have revolutionised how Gaelic games are accessed

(4) Blue screen. Laois goalkeeper Enda Rowland has mixed results with two late frees – he blasts to the net in the first minute of injury-time but, a few minutes later, his effort is blocked out for a 65 and Dublin hang on to win

16 Leinster GAA Hurling Senior Championship - Chadwicks Wexford Park, Wexford
Wexford 1-19   Galway 1-19

17 Munster GAA Hurling Senior Championship - Páirc Uí Chaoimh, Cork
Cork 1-17   Limerick 2-25

1.

2.

(1) Conor McDonald gets fired up after firing home a late goal that turned this game on its head.
With Lee Chin adding four late points for Wexford, Galway are left to wonder how they fail to get
off to a winning start in the championship

(2) Any which way. It takes a magician like Limerick's Cian Lynch to pull off a trick like this –
scoring a point while down on one knee. However, another magician, Cork's Patrick Horgan,
did exactly the same last year which – naturally – was captured for posterity in *A Season of Sundays*

17 Connacht GAA Football Senior Championship - Gaelic Park, The Bronx, New York
New York 0-15   Sligo 1-16

Munster GAA Hurling Senior Championship - Walsh Park, Waterford
Waterford 2-24   Tipperary 2-20

1.

(1) Daniel O'Sullivan gets some encouragement and consoling words from New York chairperson Joan Henchy after a battling performance against Sligo. Henchy, born in Yonkers but raised in Tarbert, has been a driving force in the New York GAA for more than two decades and one suspects it won't be long before Connacht teams start dreading this fixture

(2) A thousand eyes are one eye. Spectators follow the flight of the sliotar at Walsh Park watching and wondering – will it go between the posts, drift wide or drop short

23 Ulster GAA Football Senior Championship - Corrigan Park, Belfast
Antrim 0-10   Cavan 1-20

Leinster GAA Hurling Senior Championship - Chadwicks Wexford Park, Wexford
Wexford 0-23   Dublin 0-24

Leinster GAA Hurling Senior Championship - UPMC Nowlan Park, Kilkenny
Kilkenny 2-34   Laois 1-14

Leinster GAA Hurling Senior Championship - Pearse Stadium, Salthill
Galway 3-36   Westmeath 1-17

1.

2.

3.

4.

(1) Variously described as "an oasis in a concrete city" and "a place apart", a resplendent and renovated Corrigan Park stages Antrim's first championship match since 2013. This aerial shot of the action shows the tight confines of the Whiterock Road venue nestled in the shadow of Black Mountain

(2) Goalie on goalie. Dublin goalkeeper Seán Brennan dives full length to bat away a penalty taken by the Wexford netminder Mark Fanning, a crucial save in a tight encounter

(3) Stealing a march. Eoin Cody, another young Kilkenny player making a name for himself, shows a deft touch to get away from Laois's Seán Downey

(4) Panel effort. Galway captain Daithí Burke and his troops get the traditional slaps and claps from the other squad members as they emerge from the dressing-room

23 Munster GAA Hurling Senior Championship - TUS Gaelic Grounds, Limerick
Limerick 0-30   Waterford 2-21

24 Leinster GAA Football Senior Championship - County Grounds, Aughrim
Wicklow 5-15   Laois 4-12

Munster GAA Hurling Senior Championship - FBD Semple Stadium, Thurles
Tipperary 2-16   Clare 3-21

1.

2.

3.

(1) In the thick of it. One can't criticise the man in the middle Seán Stack for not keeping up – or down – with the play as Limerick defender Dan Morrissey moves in to lift the sliotar ahead of Waterford's Patrick Curran

(2-3) Happy days. This is a proud moment for Eugene Dooley, one of Wicklow's most prominent sponsors and supporters in recent times, having a chat with Darragh Fitzgerald after a rare championship victory – helped by a hat-trick of goals from Kevin Quinn. Meanwhile, Clare duo Peter Duggan and Ryan Taylor can relax after a job well done on Tipperary

24

Connacht GAA Football Senior Championship - Hastings Insurance MacHale Park, Castlebar
Mayo 0-16   Galway 1-14

Leinster GAA Football Senior Championship - Páirc Tailteann, Navan
Louth 5-10   Carlow 0-10

Ulster GAA Football Senior Championship - MacCumhaill Park, Ballybofey
Donegal 1-16   Armagh 0-12

Leinster GAA Football Senior Championship - Chadwicks Wexford Park, Wexford
Wexford 1-15   Offaly 1-12

1.

2.

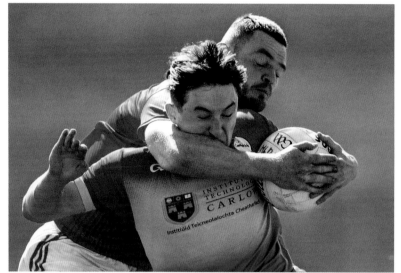

3.

4.

30 Connacht GAA Football Senior Championship - Markievicz Park, Sligo
Sligo 0-11   Roscommon 0-23

Leinster GAA Football Senior Championship - TEG Cusack Park, Mullingar
Westmeath 3-13   Longford 0-14

Munster GAA Football Senior Championship - Fraher Field, Dungarvan
Waterford 1-08   Tipperary 2-13

5.

6.

7.

(1) Just one of the crowd. Amid the well-wishers, Finnian Ó Laoí poses for a picture with his parents, Caitriona and Joe, after Galway halt a run of poor results against arch rivals Mayo. This could herald a significant power shift in Connacht

(2) The wraparound. Conor Crowley feels the brunt of a hefty tackle by Louth's Niall Sharkey, typifying a rough day for Carlow who ship five goals

(3) Michael Murphy may be a fraction late in stopping Jarly Óg Burns but he and his Donegal team-mates put a halt to Armagh's championship gallop. Temporarily

(4) Wexford players are jubilant after staging an unexpected coup against a fancied Offaly side; (5) Roscommon forward Conor Cox has a selfie taken with members of the Sharkey family, Pádraig, Seán and Jason; (6) and Westmeath's experienced campaigner John Heslin has the fist in the air after scoring his side's first goal

(7) From lean to leaner – that's how Waterford's football fortunes fluctuate but they never throw in the towel. Here Brian Looby tries to block a shot by Tipp's Mikey O'Shea

30   Munster GAA Football Senior Championship - Cusack Park, Ennis
Clare 1-19   Limerick 2-16 (Limerick win 4-1 on penalties)

Ulster GAA Football Senior Championship - St Tiernach's Park, Clones
Monaghan 0-23   Down 2-07

1.

(1) Pressure kick. Clare goalkeeper Tristan O'Callaghan tries to read Robbie Bourke's intentions as the number 26 prepares to take Limerick's second kick in the penalty shootout. It's the first time a senior championship game has been decided on penalties – and it would not be the last of the season

(2) Attention. Larry McCarthy, the president of the GAA, and Heather Humphreys, the Minister for Social Protection and Minister for Rural and Community Development, are among those standing for Amhrán na bhFiann, as Katie Boyle sings and Eunice Downey of the Mayobridge Band accompanies

1.

❝ I didn't notice any tension. The handshake happened, I didn't see anything in it ❞

Galway manager Henry Shefflin wonders at all the fuss over his somewhat awkward looking handshake with Kilkenny manager Brian Cody

(1) The most commented-upon handshake in Irish sport since Roy Keane and Mick McCarthy? This frosty exchange between the two Kilkenny greats Brian Cody and Henry Shefflin has been parsed and analysed by the amateur psychologists and experts on body language out there, but only the two managers know what was behind it all

(2) A Glass more than half-full. Derry manager Rory Gallagher reacts with unbridled joy and Conor Glass – one his big performers in an 11-point win over Tyrone – gets a special congratulation at the final whistle. This result lays down a marker

2.

1 Leinster GAA Football Senior Championship - Páirc Tailteann, Navan
Meath 4-13   Wicklow 1-12

Leinster GAA Football Senior Championship - O'Connor Park, Tullamore
Kildare 2-22   Louth 0-12

Munster GAA Hurling Senior Championship - FBD Semple Stadium, Thurles
Cork 2-20   Clare 0-28

7 Munster GAA Football Senior Championship - Páirc Uí Rinn, Cork
Cork 0-11   Kerry 0-23

" Thurles is a tough place to come to but it's where every hurler wants to play "

Clare manager Brian Lohan is pleased with the Banner's latest 'trip to Tipp' which saw them notch up a two-point win over Cork

(1-2) Meath's James McEntee hits top gear, accelerating away from Rory Stokes of Wicklow whereas Louth's Donal McKenny, left, and Ciarán Keenan look pretty fed up after losing to Kildare. Two easy victories highlight Leinster football's lack of competitiveness

(3) O'Donnell Abú. Shane O'Donnell has a word with county sponsor Pat O'Donnell, no doubt reflecting on Clare's championship resurgence – two wins out of two sets them up nicely

(4) All kitted out. There was a Newbridge-or-nowhere stand-off over the venue for this clash but with Kerry agreeing to play in Páirc Uí Rinn, three-year-old Olivia Griffin and her sister Éabha, aged five, from Dromid, get a day out in Cork – with their teddies of course

8 Munster GAA Hurling Senior Championship - TUS Gaelic Grounds, Limerick
Limerick 3-21   Tipperary 0-23

Connacht GAA Football Senior Championship - Pearse Stadium, Salthill
Galway 4-20   Leitrim 0-09

Ulster GAA Football Senior Championship - St Tiernach's Park, Clones
Donegal 2-16   Cavan 0-16

1.

2.

(1-2) All-Ireland keepy-uppy champion contenders. Gearóid Hegarty of Limerick tries his football skills out for size with a sliotar while Galway's Damien Comer gets a feel for the big ball before they go into battle – some of the tricks that two of the country's finest athletes have in their repertoire

(3) The delighted Donegal fans far outnumber the handful of dejected Cavan supporters watching the first goal, scored by Conor O'Donnell, not pictured

4.

1.

2.

14 EirGrid GAA Football All-Ireland Under-20 Championship Final - Avant Money Páirc Seán Mac Diarmada, Carrick-on-Shannon
Tyrone 1-20 Kildare 1-14

Leinster GAA Hurling Senior Championship - MW Hire O'Moore Park, Portlaoise
Laois 0-21 Galway 2-37

Munster GAA Football Senior Championship - FBD Semple Stadium, Thurles
Tipperary 0-10 Limerick 2-10

Leinster GAA Hurling Senior Championship - TEG Cusack Park, Mullingar
Westmeath 2-15 Wexford 0-21

5.

6.

(1) The Tyrone conveyer belt is still humming. This is their sixth title at under-21 or under-20 level, and some of these celebrating players could be fast-tracked to senior ranks sooner rather than later

(2) Yellow brick road. Two loyal Galway supporters await the start of a game that won't disturb their relaxed pose on the terraces

(3-4) Getting into the picture. Two youngsters taking their mascot duties seriously are four-year-old Iarla McLoughlin, applauding the Tipperary squad during the team photo, and three-year-old Oisín Craig, son of Westmeath player Aaron Craig, listening to the post-match huddle. This is a happy huddle following Westmeath's superb performance in earning a draw that proved so costly for Wexford

14 Leinster GAA Hurling Senior Championship - Parnell Park, Dublin
Dublin 0-17   Kilkenny 3-25

15 Leinster GAA Football Senior Championship - Croke Park, Dublin
Kildare 1-21   Westmeath 2-15

Munster GAA Hurling Senior Championship - Walsh Park, Waterford
Waterford 1-19   Cork 2-22

Munster GAA Hurling Senior Championship - Cusack Park, Ennis
Clare 0-24   Limerick 1-21

1.

2.

3.

(1) Brian Cody doesn't mind the cameras clicking, especially on those days when his team clicks. And Kilkenny were certainly in top form on this occasion, giving Dublin a dose of the blues in their own backyard for the second time in the space of ten weeks

(2) Organised chaos. The Westmeath footballers go through their routine before the Leinster semi-final – the pre-match drills are becoming more elaborate and complicated, and part of the day's entertainment

(3) You write off the Rebels at your peril. Cork rediscover their mojo after losing their first two championship outings, and a pumped-up Darragh Fitzgibbon is delighted to give the begrudgers their answer. Meanwhile, Waterford's form is taking the opposite trajectory, as manager Liam Cahill knows only too well: "We hurled like a car on dirty petrol, just chugging along"

(4) You can see the lighter side when the game is all over. Referee Colm Lyons and Clare centre back John Conlon share a private joke after the second draw between Limerick and the Banner this season

" We see it every single training session, he is just a phenomenal guy "

Clare manager Brian Lohan is unsurprised by the performance of his star forward Tony Kelly

15 Ulster GAA Football Senior Championship - Athletic Grounds, Armagh
Derry 3-12   Monaghan 0-17

Leinster GAA Football Senior Championship - Croke Park, Dublin
Dublin 1-27   Meath 1-14

21 Nicky Rackard Cup Final - Croke Park, Dublin
Tyrone 1-27   Roscommon 0-19

Lory Meagher Cup Final - Croke Park, Dublin
Louth 3-27   Longford 3-14

1.

2.

(1) Heart on sleeve. Rory Gallagher will never be accused of being understated but his passion is rubbing off on his Derry squad whose star continues to rise under his tutelage

(2) A Royal pain. Bryan Menton contests a dropping ball with John Small on a miserable day for Meath but an almost perfect one for Dublin who had victory wrapped up by half-time with a 15-point lead, 1-17 to 0-5

(3-4) The Nicky Rackard and Lory Meagher Cups go to Tyrone and Louth, to the great delight of Lorcan Devlin, on his knees, and captain Feidhleim Joyce with the trophy. Unfortunately, within five weeks of this success Tyrone's star performer, Damian Casey, died in a tragic accident in Spain. Tony Donnelly, the chairman of Casey's club Eoghan Ruadh, described him as "an icon of our club… he made the game look easy"

3.

4.

2.

1.

3.

4.

21 Christy Ring Cup Final - Croke Park, Dublin
Kildare 2-29   Mayo 0-19

Tailteann Cup - County Grounds, Aughrim
Wicklow 3-16   Waterford 1-10

Leinster GAA Hurling Senior Championship - Pearse Stadium, Salthill
Galway 0-27   Dublin 0-21

22 Leinster GAA Hurling Senior Championship - UPMC Nowlan Park, Kilkenny
Kilkenny 1-18   Wexford 1-22

oneills.com GAA Hurling All-Ireland Under-20 Championship Final - FBD Semple Stadium, Thurles
Kilkenny 0-19   Limerick 0-18

Munster GAA Hurling Senior Championship - FBD Semple Stadium, Thurles
Tipperary 1-24   Cork 3-30

5.

6.

(1) Moving up in the world. Kildare's hurling stock continues to rise with this Christy Ring Cup success, and it's on to the Joe McDonagh Cup competition in 2023

(2-4) It's the end of the road for the Waterford footballers and the Dublin hurlers and a bump on the road for Kilkenny's hurlers. The Déise's Conor Murray is dejected after defeat to Wicklow; Galway's Conor Whelan signs his way through a phalanx of hurleys and autograph hunters after Galway finish off Dublin; and the legendary Eddie Keher – looking fit and healthy at 80 – lines up a free as part of a Kilkenny GAA Supporters Club fundraiser in aid of the Irish Red Cross Ukraine Appeal at half-time in a home defeat

(5) The general assumption is that Kilkenny are continually hoovering up All-Ireland titles at all grades but, in fact, this is their first at under-21/under-20 level since 2008. Eoghan O'Brien, wearing 18, Ted Dunne (21) and Paddy Langton (7) won't pay too much attention to what the record books say

(6) Cork put the final nail in Tipp's coffin – making it four championship defeats out of four – and save their own season, although Ronan Maher, left, and Séamus Kennedy make Shane Kingston and his team-mates work for everything

1.

2.

(1) A drafty dugout. Offaly manager John Maughan is the super sub sitting in the Enniscorthy rust belt, where ventilation won't be an issue

(2) Falling off the wagon. From league winners to championship also-rans, Waterford are the big casualties in the rough and tumble of the Munster championship as Clare's Peter Duggan, supported by Robin Mounsey, is tackled by Ian Kenny and Conor Gleeson, right

(3) Dress to impress. This spectator has wisely brought some protection against the sun while brightening up the grey terraces in Fitzgerald Stadium, but his colour scheme gives no clue about where his allegiances lie

(4) A headscratcher. This defeat is the last match of James McCartan's second stint as Down manager so the post-mortem with county board secretary Seán Óg McAteer will be brief. However, McCartan may give some thought to the oddities of the modern game, in particular how a goalkeeper – in this case, Cavan's Raymond Gallagher with seven points – ends up as the leading scorer

4.

28 Tailteann Cup - Glennon Brothers Pearse Park, Longford
Longford 0-12   Fermanagh 1-12

Tailteann Cup - Markievicz Park, Sligo
Sligo 3-15   London 2-16

Leinster GAA Football Senior Championship Final - Croke Park, Dublin
Dublin 5-17   Kildare 1-15

1.

2.

(1) James McMahon tracks the run of Longford's Dessie Reynolds with Fermanagh
advancing to the Tailteann Cup semi-finals thanks to Ultan Kelm's decisive goal

(2) Taking the learnings. London manager Michael Maher is no doubt reminding his
players that some positives can be taken from this narrow defeat, with Sligo pushed all
the way and having to rely on goalkeeper Aidan Devaney to save a penalty in extra-time

(3) A special occasion for St Oliver Plunkett Eoghan Ruadh with one of their own,
Seán Bugler, posing with the club's under-11 players and the Delaney Cup in Croke Park.
Darragh McMahon, Senan O'Reilly, Charlie Franzoni, Conor Hayes, Alex Moore, Zach
Guemmour, Aidan Doohan, Jason Donnelly, Alex O'Brien-Moore, Zach Hughes, Hugo
Murphy, Alfie Leddy and Cian Dodrill have just seen their heroes stun Kildare with five
goals in 26 minutes and annex a 12th successive Leinster title

29 Tailteann Cup - MW Hire O'Moore Park, Portlaoise
Laois 0-13   Westmeath 1-13

Ulster GAA Football Senior Championship Final - St Tiernach's Park, Clones
Derry 1-16   Donegal 1-14

1.

(1) If you're good enough, you're old enough. Still competing at
39, having started with the Laois seniors in 2003, Ross Munnelly's
attitude is: "I don't think motivation should be a problem with any
player." After coming on as a substitute, Ross is photographed
with his mother Mary

(2) Out of the shadows in Ulster. In the battle of the blanket
defences, Derry's durability eventually pays off in extra-time and
their players, from left, Paul McNeill, Shea Downey, Conor Glass
and Emmett Bradley bask in the achievement of bringing home
the county's first provincial title in 24 years

1.

2.

3.

❝ He is one of the best footballers I have ever seen playing but Shane knows himself that he has to produce these performances in the big games. That way he will get more national recognition ❞

Galway football manager Pádraic Joyce is delighted with Shane Walsh's Connacht final display

29 Tailteann Cup - O'Connor Park, Tullamore
Offaly 0-18   Wicklow 0-10

Connacht GAA Football Senior Championship Final - Pearse Stadium, Salthill
Galway 2-19   Roscommon 2-16

4 GAA Football All-Ireland Senior Championship Qualifiers Round 1 - Páirc Uí Chaoimh, Cork
Cork 2-12   Louth 2-08

GAA Football All-Ireland Senior Championship Qualifiers Round 1 - Hastings Insurance MacHale Park, Castlebar
Mayo 1-13   Monaghan 0-12

4.

(1) Not exactly a helping hand. Hitting the ground, Offaly's Rory Egan looks like he's performing a pilates or yoga exercise following an unorthodox tackle by Patrick O'Keane of Wicklow

(2) Out of the West. Tomo Culhane, Johnny Heaney and Owen Gallagher celebrate with the Nestor Cup as Galway become top dogs in Connacht again, earning their first title since 2018. The maroon resurgence under manager Pádraic Joyce gathers pace

(3) That familiar stride. Another game, another sideline, Louth manager Mickey Harte walks to a position he has occupied thousands of times in his long career

(4) Back in their droves. The Mayo – and Monaghan – faithful turn out to witness the big tie in round one of the qualifiers. Mayo advance which leads to another manager biting the dust, Séamus Banty McEnaney ending his second tenure at the helm in Monaghan

4 Tailteann Cup - O'Connor Park, Tullamore
Offaly 3-17 New York 0-11

Joe McDonagh Cup Final -Croke Park, Dublin
Antrim 5-22 Kerry 4-24

1. 2.

(1) The Exiles return. More football games for New York and exposure to different teams is one of the benefits of the Tailteann Cup, particularly as they missed the last two Connacht campaigns because of Covid. Manager Johnny McGeeney, an Armagh native, outlines the strategy in the O'Connor Park dressing-room

(2) Thrill-a-minute. James McNaughton is fired up after scoring his side's second goal in the 10th minute and Antrim get off to a flier in a sensational Joe McDonagh Cup final. Then Kerry turn the tables after the interval and emulate Antrim's first-half tally of 3-14, leaving the winning manager Darren Gleeson – not to mention fans of the teams – feeling "numb" at the end

4 Leinster GAA Hurling Senior Championship Final - Croke Park, Dublin
Kilkenny 0-22   Galway 0-17

GAA Football All-Ireland Senior Championship Qualifiers Round 1 - Cusack Park, Ennis
Clare 1-11   Meath 1-09

5 GAA Football All-Ireland Senior Championship Qualifiers Round 1 - Athletic Grounds, Armagh
Armagh 1-16   Tyrone 1-10

Tailteann Cup - Avant Money Páirc Seán Mac Diarmada, Carrick-on-Shannon
Leitrim 2-16   Sligo 1-19 (Sligo win 4-3 on penalties)

" Dealing with success is not easy and we saw that all year. We will just have to review it and see if there is something we can identify **"**

Tyrone joint-manager Feargal Logan puzzles over a very disappointing year for the reigning All-Ireland football champions which ends with a defeat to arch rivals Armagh

1.

2.

3.

(1) An in-joke. Kilkenny goalkeeper Eoin Murphy cracks up following some witticism from big Walter Walsh, left, or Cian Kenny

(2) Making an entrance, making an exit. Andy McEntee, entering the pitch at Cusack Park before his team's defeat, steps down as Meath manager a few days later, thus ending a six-year stint. But he's not out of a job for long as he accepts the Antrim post five weeks later, commenting: "I'm sure this surprises a lot of people but it probably surprises me as much as anybody else"

(3) One of the stars of the season. Rian O'Neill is once again imperious as Armagh beat their great rivals Tyrone for the third time this season, the All-Ireland champions bowing out not with a bang but with a whimper

(4) You de man. Penalty shootouts invariably turn goalkeepers into heroes and Sligo's Aidan Devaney is the one who steps up to the plate against Leitrim, saving two spot-kicks in the shootout and then being mobbed by his jubilant team-mates

4.

1.

2.

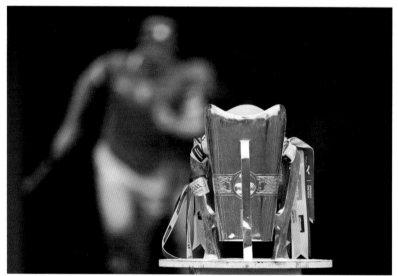

3.

4.

5 Munster GAA Hurling Senior Championship Final - FBD Semple Stadium, Thurles
Limerick 1-29 Clare 0-29

5.

6.

(1) Come early and come prepared. Clare supporters Mary Gallagher, left, with Brid and Johnny McMahon from Kilkishen wait with their bags packed for the Semple Stadium turnstiles to open before the Munster hurling final

(2) Tuning up. Artane Band members Matthew Newell, left, and Thomas Kilbane get ready in the tunnel before performing Amhrán na bhFiann

(3) In the footsteps of a hurling giant. How appropriate that Limerick, led by their captain Declan Hannon, are the first winners of the Mick Mackey Cup which replaced the Munster Senior Hurling Cup this year. Mackey was a star in the 1930s and 40s during Limerick's first golden age, winning three All-Ireland senior medals and five Munster medals

(4-5) An almighty battle, an epic, one of the greatest Munster finals, this clash went down to the wire, even in extra-time. Giving a flavour of the action, Clare's Diarmuid Ryan gets to grips with Tom Morrissey whose Limerick team-mate Gearóid Hegarty celebrates after a classy goal. The pecking order in Munster has been turned on its head completely as this is the Treaty's fourth provincial title in a row

(6) The Abs store. The Limerick body building club of, from left, Nickie Quaid, Seán Finn, Mike Casey, Peter Nash and Diarmaid Byrnes flex their muscles after putting their bodies on the line

11

GAA Football All-Ireland Senior Championship Qualifiers Round 2 - Croke Park, Dublin
Clare 2-15   Roscommon 1-17

GAA Hurling All-Ireland Senior Championship Preliminary Quarter-Final - Austin Stack Park, Tralee
Kerry 0-18   Wexford 3-30

GAA Football All-Ireland Senior Championship Qualifiers Round 2 - Croke Park, Dublin
Mayo 2-13   Kildare 0-14

GAA Hurling All-Ireland Senior Championship Preliminary Quarter-Final - Corrigan Park, Belfast
Antrim 2-19   Cork 3-27

1.

2.

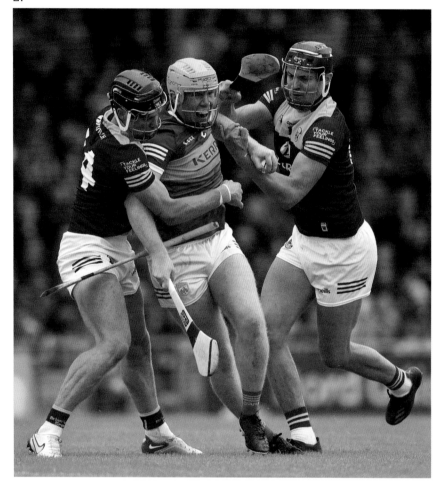

(1) Special moment. Keelan Sexton gets a big hug from his parents, Kevin and Sinéad, after contributing hugely to Clare's comeback against Roscommon with a 2-6 haul

(2) Stepping up a level. Kerry and Antrim's reward for reaching the Joe McDonagh Cup final is a date with home venue against two of the big guns, Wexford and Cork. But the big guns don't take any prisoners, as Kerry's Conor O'Keeffe discovers against Conor McDonald and Jack O'Connor of Wexford

(3) After the pummelling they got from Dublin in the Leinster final, Kildare prove much more resilient and sticky opponents against Mayo, but the end result is the same. Fergal Conway feels the pain of defeat

(4) Any vantage point will do. Commentator Oisín Langan, right, calls the action at Corrigan Park for GAAGO, the video streaming service developed by the GAA and RTÉ so that fans around the world can watch the games via the internet

" That was bad for the heart. I am very proud of the players, they're a tremendous bunch of lads "

Clare football manager Colm Collins catches his breath following his side's late, come-from-behind, one-point victory over Roscommon at Croke Park

4.

12   GAA Football All-Ireland Senior Championship Qualifiers Round 2 - St Tiernach's Park, Clones
Armagh 3-17   Donegal 0-16

18   GAA Hurling All-Ireland Senior Championship Quarter-Final - FBD Semple Stadium, Thurles
Galway 2-19   Cork 1-21

  GAA Hurling All-Ireland Senior Championship Quarter-Final - FBD Semple Stadium, Thurles
Clare 1-24   Wexford 3-14

19   Tailteann Cup Semi-Final - Croke Park, Dublin
Cavan 0-20   Sligo 1-14

  Tailteann Cup Semi-Final - Croke Park, Dublin
Westmeath 3-22   Offaly 2-16

1.

(1) Quick out of the traps. In one of the fastest goals of the season, Armagh's Rory Grugan lashes the ball to the Donegal net after just 10 seconds, a textbook finish to a move that probably came straight from the training ground. The Ulster championship setback in Ballybofey is put to rights and Armagh are on the road to Croke Park

(2) Upwards and onwards. Henry Shefflin is bringing Galway closer to where he wants them to be thanks to a narrow win over Cork – toughing it out in the tight matches is particularly heartening

(3) The Kellys' hero. When you have somebody famous in the family never let an opportunity slip to get a picture taken, which is what Kenneth Kelly and his daughter Keela are doing with the great Tony Kelly alongside fellow Clare players Jack Browne and David Fitzgerald. All in top form after dispatching Wexford

(4-5) Bedding in. The popularity of the inaugural Tailteann Cup continues to grow and the commitment of the players is evident in Cavan midfielder Thomas Galligan's jersey-pull attempt to halt Sligo's Pat Spillane and the delight on the faces of Westmeath duo Ronan O'Toole, left, and Luke Loughlin after a thumping win over neighbours Offaly

> **" I am just thrilled with the character the lads showed because it could easily have gone against us today. In some big moments big players stood up "**
>
> Galway manager Henry Shefflin is proud of the way his charges overcame the Cork challenge in the All-Ireland quarter-final

2.

3.

4.

5.

25 GAA Football All-Ireland Senior Championship Quarter-Final - Croke Park, Dublin
Derry 5-13   Clare 2-08

GAA Football All-Ireland Senior Championship Quarter-Final - Croke Park, Dublin
Dublin 0-21   Cork 0-10

1.

2.

(1) A goalfest, and a goal machine. Paul Cassidy of Derry drills home his team's third goal but, disappointingly for the neutral spectator, this is a one-sided goalfest as Derry score five of the seven. Goals are Derry's currency this season and it's now ten from their four championship matches thus far

(2) After the five-goal blitz against Kildare this is death by 21 cuts as Spectacular Dublin gives way to Efficient Dublin. It's all too much for the Leesiders with Kevin O'Donovan, trying to pass to Seán Powter, being hounded by Cormac Costello, Niall Scully and Brian Fenton

26 GAA Football All-Ireland Senior Championship Quarter-Final - Croke Park, Dublin
Galway 2-21 Armagh 3-18 (Galway win 4-1 on penalties)

1.

2.

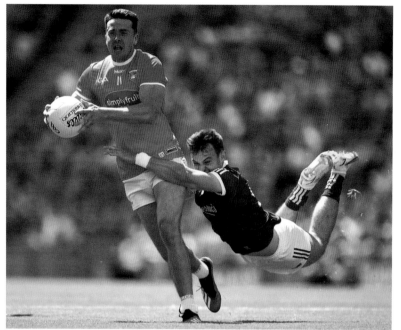

3.

4.

This game has everything, and more. This is the match the championship has been waiting for – 90 minutes of goals, incidents, comebacks, all culminating in a penalty shootout, the first ever in Croke Park: (1) Armagh bring a huge crowd for their quarter-final against Galway but, as they line up outside the stadium, few could have predicted the drama that lay in store; (2) Cillian McDaid takes to the air in an effort to thwart the run of Armagh's Stefan Campbell; (3) goalkeeper Conor Gleeson comes under pressure from Ben Crealey as Armagh's long-ball tactic causes mayhem in the Galway square during a hectic finish to normal time; (4) Matthew Tierney calmly converts his side's fourth and winning penalty in the shootout; (5) cue the euphoric rush to congratulate Tierney; (6) Galway manager Pádraic Joyce gets a sibling seal of approval from his sister Carol on a day of extraordinary events

5.

6.

❝ Penalties are for soccer not for GAA in my eyes. Fair play to both sets of players who took the penalties but it's a pure lottery. While we'll take the victory my heart goes out to Armagh ❞

Although they came out on the winning side Galway manager Pádraic Joyce is no fan of shootouts

26 GAA Football All-Ireland Senior Championship Quarter-Final - Croke Park, Dublin
Kerry 1-18   Mayo 0-13

2 GAA Hurling All-Ireland Senior Championship Semi-Final - Croke Park, Dublin
Kilkenny 2-26   Clare 0-20

(1) Management can get you down. For the last time, James Horan takes up his position on the sideline for a big match but defeat leads to a quick decision to step down and end his second term as Mayo boss. He is one of many high-profile football managers to do so this summer after the departures of men like Declan Bonner in Donegal, Séamus McEnaney (Monaghan), James McCartan (Down), Andy McEntee (Meath), Anthony Cunningham (Roscommon), Keith Ricken (Cork), John Maughan (Offaly) and Enda McGinley (Antrim)

(2) Basking in an amber glow. This magnificent study could be a promotion shot about hurling giants, although goalkeeper Eoin Murphy and Kilkenny are only focused on reaching the All-Ireland decider with a masterclass in precision play

1.

2.

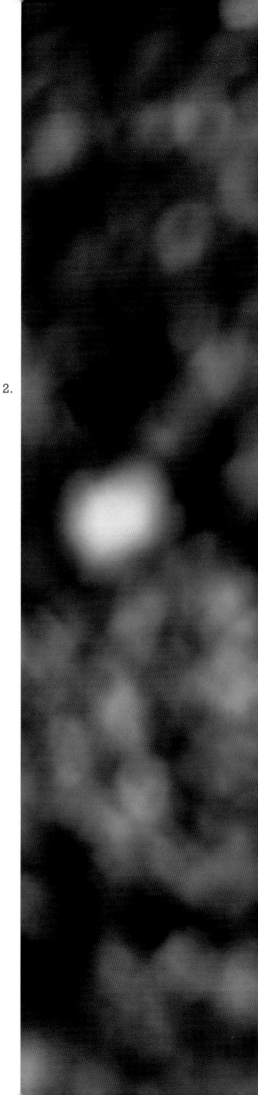

❝ We had an awful lot of possession but just didn't get the return from our attacks. Kerry certainly did and that was the difference ❞

A disappointed Mayo manager James Horan summarises what proves to be his last match in charge of his native county

3 Electric Ireland GAA Hurling All-Ireland Minor Championship Final - UPMC Nowlan Park, Kilkenny
Tipperary 1-17   Offaly 1-16

GAA Hurling All-Ireland Senior Championship Semi-Final - Croke Park, Dublin
Limerick 0-27   Galway 1-21

1.

2.

(1) A minor classic. This is possibly the happiest group of players on these pages, and with good reason. Tipperary complete a roller-coaster journey to the title with a winning goal in the fifth minute of injury-time that leaves Offaly shattered and an attendance of over 27,000 utterly enthralled. Never-say-die Tipp thus take their first All-Ireland minor title since 2016 and 21st in all

(2) Early birds. The sense of expectation – and perhaps apprehension – can be detected on the faces of Limerick and Galway supporters waiting for the turnstiles to open on Jones' Road before the All-Ireland hurling semi-final

3 GAA Hurling All-Ireland Senior Championship Semi-Final - Croke Park, Dublin
Limerick 0-27 Galway 1-21

1.

(1) On the front foot. Not for the first time during the season, Limerick's Kyle Hayes is out in front and the one to chase down, the man of the match putting on the after-burners and leaving Galway players scrambling, from left, Darren Morrissey, Cathal Mannion, Jack Grealish and Ronan Glennon

(2) Lingering in his goalmouth, goalkeeper Éanna Murphy looks down an emptying pitch wondering what more Galway could have done but knowing also that they gave their best against the reigning All-Ireland champions. Limerick are not a great team for nothing

2.

❝ We got off to a good start and were in flow very early but that flow got disrupted. Galway got back into the game, settled, started getting some fluency going themselves, and it was nip and tuck. Ultimately it came down to the final quarter, which we won. That was the vital part **❞**

Limerick hurling manager John Kiely sums up their hard-fought semi-final victory over Galway

8 Electric Ireland GAA Football All-Ireland Minor Championship Final - Dr Hyde Park, Roscommon
Galway 0-15 Mayo 0-09

9 Tailteann Cup Final - Croke Park, Dublin
Cavan 1-13 Westmeath 2-14

3.

1.

2.

(1) Third time lucky. Galway lost twice to Mayo in this year's minor football championship and three games overall but in the end they're the ones holding the Tom Markham Cup, having saved their best till last. This turnaround is a bitter pill to swallow for Mayo who lost only one match all season – the most important one

Westmeath will go into the history books as the first winners of the Tailteann Cup: (2) Mobilising. Young Westmeath supporters turn out in force for the final against Cavan at Croke Park; (3) Up and running. Lorcan Dolan celebrates his 28th-minute goal as the Westmeath challenge moves up through the gears; (4) No half measures. Captain Kevin Maguire raises the Tailteann Cup for the first time as the success is celebrated lustily and comments afterwards. "I think we've really gained from this competition … it's something that really matters." It certainly matters to the supporters who turn out in their thousands in Mullingar to give the players a proper welcome home

9 TG4 All-Ireland Ladies Football Senior Championship Quarter-Final - Avant Money Páirc Seán Mac Diarmada, Carrick-on-Shannon
Dublin 1-07   Donegal 3-07

TG4 All-Ireland Ladies Football Senior Championship Quarter-Final - O'Connor Park, Tullamore
Meath 1-12   Galway 1-11

TG4 All-Ireland Ladies Football Senior Championship Quarter-Final - O'Connor Park, Tullamore
Armagh 2-14   Kerry 4-12

TG4 All-Ireland Ladies Football Senior Championship Quarter-Final - Cusack Park, Ennis
Cork 0-17   Mayo 2-13

2.

1.

The odd woman out. Unfortunately, (4) Cork's Emma Cleary is the only player experiencing the disappointment of defeat in these shots. In contrast, (1) Niamh McLaughlin, the former Ireland under-19 soccer international celebrating Donegal's big shock of the season in eliminating Dublin,(2) the indefatigable Meath duo of Orlagh Lally, left, and Emma Duggan and (3) Kerry's trio of Cáit Lynch, left, Louise Galvin in the centre and Niamh Ní Chonchúir move on to the semi-finals after four competitive encounters

3.

4.

9 GAA Football All-Ireland Senior Championship Semi-Final - Croke Park, Dublin
Galway 2-08   Derry 1-06

1.

2.

(1) HawkEye returns a false negative. There may have been a virus in the system when the technology rules out Shane Walsh's perfectly accurate 45 in the 38th minute, a decision that is reversed at half-time. As Galway manager Pádraic Joyce muses afterwards: "Technology is human too, maybe." Walsh also has the difficulty of negotiating Derry's windmill defending at free-kicks

(2) Arrowed to perfection. Damien Comer capitalises on the absence of Derry goalkeeper Odhran Lynch to finish exquisitely from long distance, the Galwayman's shot hitting the net without bouncing. With Lynch ignoring the age-old warning to mind your house, this goal was coming but it still takes a sublime piece of skill to execute it

" We were beaten by a better team, no doubt about it "

A forthright assessment by Derry manager Rory Gallagher after their semi-final defeat

9 GAA Football All-Ireland Senior Championship Semi-Final - Croke Park, Dublin
Galway 2-08 Derry 1-06

(1-2) Maroon magic. Damien Comer is one of the driving forces in Galway's march to their first All-Ireland final since 2001 and he also scores the Tribesmen's first goal against Derry, a big moment in a tight game which he acknowledges whole-heartedly. Also celebrating their ticket to the final are substitute Dessie Conneely and Dylan McHugh

1.   2.

10   GAA Football All-Ireland Junior Championship Final - Croke Park, Dublin
Kilkenny 3-12   New York 1-09

GAA Football All-Ireland Senior Championship Semi-Final - Croke Park, Dublin
Dublin 1-13   Kerry 1-14

1.   2.

(1) Who knew? Kilkenny *can* play football and, to prove it, they rock up to Croke
Park and win the All-Ireland junior championship for the first time – what's rare
is wonderful. Afterwards, captain Mick Malone and his team, which included
four-time hurling All Star Paul Murphy at full back, assemble for a historic photo

(2) The atmosphere and the added frisson when Dublin and Kerry meet at this
time of the year are captured here as supporters in the Cusack Stand get in the
mood early for the clash of the game's heavyweights

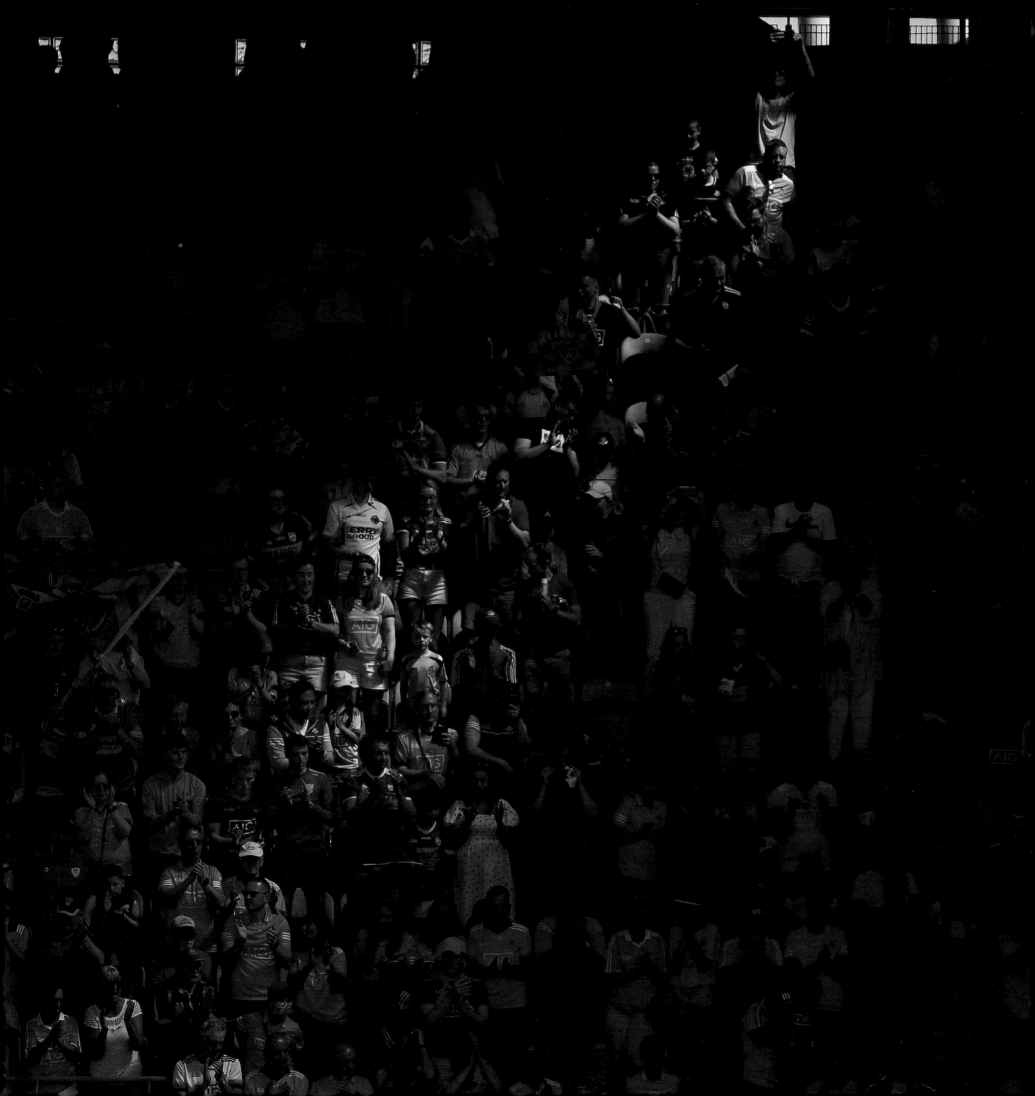

1.

2.

3.

4.

(1) Declaration of intent. Kerry seize the early initiative when Seanie O'Shea takes advantage of some hesitancy in the Dublin defence and slips the ball under goalkeeper Evan Comerford after just four minutes

(2-3) Possession is priceless between two teams so comfortable on the ball with Kerry's Diarmuid O'Connor determined to evade Lorcan O'Dell's tackle and Eoin Murchan's pace getting him to the ball ahead of Paul Geaney

(3) Momentum shift. Seanie O'Shea has a golden opportunity to add to his early goal but his penalty is easily saved by Evan Comerford. So begins a thorough search of the Kerry psyche – it doesn't pay to give Dublin a lifeline

1.

" I didn't think it was kickable to be honest. That has to be one of the best pressure kicks we have seen in Croke Park in a long, long time **"**

As with everyone else who witnessed it, both live and on TV, Kerry manager Jack O'Connor is mightily impressed with Seanie O'Shea's winning point

2.

(1) One for the ages. Seanie O'Shea reaches deep into his well-stocked locker of skills to pull out a sublime extra-time winning point from a free, one of the great pressure scores in championship history. Kicking into the wind and into Hill 16, his booming effort is still climbing as it clears the Dublin crossbar. Even his manager Jack O'Connor didn't believe it was kickable – "I didn't think a man could get that distance because Seanie O'Shea had emptied the tank" – but as this sequence demonstrates, O'Shea trusts his technique totally. It's like 2011 in reverse when Kerry were famously denied by Stephen Cluxton's last-minute free

(2) Seconds later it's all over, and referee Paddy Neilan's full-time whistle signals high jinks from Seanie O'Shea, Killian Spillane, left, and Adrian Spillane. Kerry have shifted a monkey off their backs as they hadn't beaten Dublin in the championship in five attempts since 2009

1.

2.

That ring of confidence. The big beaming faces and smiling eyes of (1) Meath players
Niamh O'Sullivan, left, and Monica McGuirk and (2) the Kerry duo of Niamh Carmody, left,
and Clódagh Ní Chonchúir tell you that these teams will contest the ladies football final

17 GAA Hurling All-Ireland Senior Championship Final - Croke Park, Dublin
Limerick 1-31 Kilkenny 2-26

1.   2.

(1) Start them young. Max Melbourne, aged one and a half, sports the Limerick colours in the hours before the All-Ireland hurling final

(2) May the force be with you. GAA president Larry McCarthy wishes referee Colm Lyons well before the final, reinforcing the message of respect for match officials

17 GAA Hurling All-Ireland Senior Championship Final - Croke Park, Dublin
Limerick 1-31 Kilkenny 2-26

" According to most people's predictions we weren't at the level of even getting to an All-Ireland final. But I think our players deserve fantastic admiration for the way they fought it out "

Kilkenny manager Brian Cody

1.

3.

(1) The exuberant hop, skip and a jump from Eoin Cody followed by Martin Keoghan (14) and Conor Browne running past the Liam MacCarthy Cup herald Kilkenny's entry to the Croke Park arena

(2) One step removed. Luck doesn't smile on Cian Lynch who injures his ankle in training just seven days before the biggest game of the year, but the 2021 Hurler of the Year still plays a hugely influential role in the background in the run-up to the final and on the day

(3) Declan Hannon will need a deft touch to control the sliotar to fend off Billy Ryan's equally deft use of his hurley

2.

(1) Spellbound. Rapt. Transfixed. Limerick's Jolly Green Army dominate this section of the Croke Park crowd, eyes glued to events on the field in an enthralling final played in scorching heat

(2) Made for the big occasion. All-Ireland finals bring out the absolute best in Gearóid Hegarty who follows his returns of 0-7 in 2020 and 2-2 last year with 1-5 this time in another command performance. After savouring his sensational goal in the fourth minute it's on to the next play

17 GAA Hurling All-Ireland Senior Championship Final - Croke Park, Dublin
Limerick 1-31   Kilkenny 2-26

1.

(1-2) In a clash of titans, the battle of the skies is intense. TJ Reid, with ball in hand, tries to get away from Declan Hannon, left, and Seán Finn while Mike Casey, left, seems to get the first touch as he and fellow defender Barry Nash tag-team Walter Walsh, with Martin Keoghan ready to pounce on a break

(3) The last few minutes. Nobody celebrates prematurely against Kilkenny so it's a test of nerves for Limerick County Board chairman John Cregan, seated right, substitute goalkeeper Barry Hennessy, kitman Ger O'Connell, assistant goalkeeper coach Alan Feely and nutritionist Eoin Murray

17 GAA Hurling All-Ireland Senior Championship Final - Croke Park, Dublin
Limerick 1-31   Kilkenny 2-26

1.

2.

3.

4.

(1-3) Let the celebrations begin. Limerick supporters are getting into party mode following a late Gearóid Hegarty point; Diarmaid Byrnes, whose 36 points from long range in the championship are a huge weapon in Limerick's arsenal, and Aaron Gillane react to the final whistle; and substitute Richie English catches up with a delighted Will O'Donoghue

(4) They gave it everything. TJ Reid, with substitute Alan Murphy, leaves nothing on the pitch but has to take a back seat while the applause rings out for the winners

17 GAA Hurling All-Ireland Senior Championship Final - Croke Park, Dublin
Limerick 1-31 Kilkenny 2-26

(1) Not many teams score 2-26 against Limerick and find that it's not good enough, something a dejected Kilkenny goalkeeper Eoin Murphy and selector Martin Comerford are trying to figure out

(2) Declan Hannon becomes the first player to lift the Liam MacCarthy Cup on four occasions and, inspirational leader that he is, he makes sure that injured vice-captain Cian Lynch shares the stage with him. This is Limerick's third title in a row, their fourth in five years, 11th in all, and already this team is regarded as one of hurling's greatest

1.

2.

" Absolutely incredible. We have two or three years' worth of celebrating to catch up on "

Limerick captain Declan Hannon

17 GAA Hurling All-Ireland Senior Championship Final - Croke Park, Dublin
Limerick 1-31   Kilkenny 2-26

" Brian Cody has informed Kilkenny County Board that he is stepping down as Kilkenny Senior Hurling Team Manager. Appointed in November 1998 Brian has led the Kilkenny team to unprecedented provincial and national success and is regarded as the greatest manager in the history of hurling "

Conor Denieffe, Rúnaí Choiste
Cill Chainnigh

The end of an era. The most successful manager in the history of the game, Brian Cody, walks down the Croke Park tunnel for the last time – he announces his departure in his usual dignified, non-fussy way six days later. In his 24 years in charge, Kilkenny won 11 All-Ireland titles, 18 Leinster titles, 10 National Leagues and reached 17 All-Ireland finals. Beat that. His legacy will live on because, in TJ Reid's words, "he built an empire of spirit"

24 GAA Football All-Ireland Senior Championship Final - Croke Park, Dublin
Kerry 0-20   Galway 0-16

1.

(1) Set up for the day. Heeding Napoleon's advice that an army marches on its stomach, Galway supporters Micheál Ó Máille, left, Seán Mac Donncha, Micheál Mac Donncha and Connie Guidera, from Carraroe, tuck into a hearty breakfast in Monck's Green on Phibsborough Road on the morning of the All-Ireland football final

(2) A little spice makes all the difference. Croke Park's deputy head groundsman Colm Daly adds the final touches to the hallowed turf

(3) Pleasantries – for now. The Kerry and Galway players shake hands in the last red-carpet formality before the parade

2.

3.

1.

(1) The art of the block. After a gut-busting run to help his defence, Stephen O'Brien manages to stop Johnny Heaney's shot at goal in the 10th minute. With Galway making an impressive start, O'Brien's tracking back limits the damage

(2) They're not going to agree on this one. David Clifford grimaces after referee Seán Hurson informs him that his challenge on Galway full back Seán Kelly merits a yellow card

2.

(1-2) Warning: artists at work. A magnificent game is embellished by
two of the greatest individual displays witnessed in an All-Ireland final
– from David Clifford, who struck eight points, and Shane Walsh on the
losing side giving an unforgettable exhibition that yields nine points.
John Daly and Tom O'Sullivan strive might and main to block their
distinctive kicking actions

1.

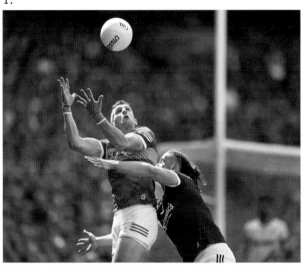

2.

3.

(1-2) In a final that ebbs and flows, Paul Geaney times his catch ahead of Kieran Molloy and calls a mark which he points, while the tireless Paudie Clifford protects the ball under pressure from Jack Glynn

(3) The man with the Midas touch. Jack O'Connor's brief when reappointed by Kerry in 2021 was simple – win an All-Ireland title, nothing more, nothing less – and he delivers in his first year. It's the fourth senior success for the Kingdom under his management

(4) A parallel universe only feet away. The final whistle is the moment when David Clifford and Seanie O'Shea can celebrate the scaling of Gaelic football's Everest but for John Daly, left, and Liam Silke the feeling is decidedly different

4.

" It's very hard to put my feeling into words – it's something I've dreamt of all my life. I was always confident we would get over the line but it was unbelievable to hear the way the crowd got behind us in the second half **"**

Kerry's star man, David Clifford, after winning his first All-Ireland senior medal

1.

2.

(1) Beidh lá eile ag an bPaorach. Galway manager Pádraic Joyce puts on a brave face consoling his son Charlie but he himself will be consoled by the fact that Galway are a force to be reckoned with once more

(2) Top dogs again. There is no disguising Seanie O'Shea's delight as the Sam Maguire Cup is raised and booked for travel to the Kingdom for the first time since 2014. It could be the springboard for this young team to add to Kerry's 38 titles with David Clifford saying: "There definitely is a realisation that this isn't the end of us by any means, we are just getting started"

(3) This one's for the fans. The victory parade would not be complete without presenting Sam Maguire to supporters on Hill 16, with Joe O'Connor acting as cheerleader

3.

1.

2.

(1) Jack O'Connor is hoisted aloft with the cup, underlining the special bond between him and his players, some of whom he managed to a minor All-Ireland in 2014. Learning to grind out results was high on O'Connor's priorities this year plus addressing the mental side of the game: "I just think we needed everything in the end to get over the line"

(2) So close. Level with just three minutes of normal time to go and, before you know it, you're watching the presentation – Galway's Tomo Culhane, left, and Johnny Heaney digest the impact of the small margins

31 TG4 All-Ireland Ladies Football Intermediate Championship Final - Croke Park, Dublin
Laois 1-13   Wexford 1-11

TG4 All-Ireland Ladies Football Senior Championship Final - Croke Park, Dublin
Meath 3-10   Kerry 1-07

1.

2.

3.

" I am an absolute emotional wreck. I cannot put into words what today means. We have worked so hard. It's been 20 long years coming, but we did it **"**

Player of the match Aisling Donoher after Laois's win in the intermediate final

4.

(1) Clodagh Dunne from Ballyroan is the Laois player being urged on enthusiastically by her clubmates in the intermediate final, that's Clodagh Dunne the artist. Not the sort of talent that can be bought on DoneDeal

(2) Doubled up. Orlagh Kehoe of Wexford has her options limited by the combined tackle of Laois players Eva Galvin, left, and Emma Lawlor

(3) Laois captain Aimee Kelly lifts the Mary Quinn Memorial Cup, a triumph based on a gritty defensive display and a match-winning turn from Mo Nerney who scored 1-5. Nerney was also around in 2001 when Laois won their only senior All-Ireland title – she was the mascot on that occasion

(4) The 2022 senior final gets under way, with referee Maggie Farrelly throwing up the ball and Meath players Máire O'Shaughnessy, front, and Vikki Wall matching up against Lorraine Scanlon, front, and Emma Costello of Kerry

1.

2.

3.

4.

5.

" They are an awesome bunch of players.
I love them all so much **"**

Meath ladies football manager Eamonn Murray

6.

7.

(1-2) Straight from the coaching manual. Meath star Emma Duggan has the textbook striking action in shooting for goal, with Kerry's Ciara Murphy attempting to block, and there are more classic skills as Orlagh Lally, left, and Emma Costello show their athleticism under the dropping ball

(3) "You can't get any better...What a game, what a performance and two in-a-row, who would have believed it." Niamh O'Sullivan, the player of the match with 1-2, clenches her fist after kicking a late point

(4-6) Different jokes for different folks. Orlagh Lally is all smiles in the company of an emotional Meath manager Eamonn Murray; Aoibheann Leahy, who had to leave the field injured in the first half, is carried back out by her sister Ailbhe, left, and Niamh Gallogly; and captain Shauna Ennis doesn't look convinced that this is actually happening as she gears up to accept the Brendan Martin Cup for the second year in succession

(7) The last time this group will be together. There will be some changes to the Meath panel in 2023 with the departure of three of their best players – Orlagh Lally and Vikki Wall who are bound for Australia and the AFLW and Emma Troy who will be unavailable. Also leaving is the key man in their backroom team, coach Paul Garrigan

7 Glen Dimplex All-Ireland Senior Camogie Championship Final - Croke Park, Dublin
Kilkenny 1-13   Cork 1-12

1.

2.

 It's just unbelievable to have won that match. It was nip and tuck and I was sure it was heading for a replay. We had a great start but Cork kept plugging away like the great team that they are 〞

A relieved and delighted Kilkenny camogie manager Brian Dowling

3.

4.

(1) Eyes locked on. Katie Nolan, the leader of the Kilkenny attack and player of the match, is put under immense pressure by Cork newcomer Meabh Murphy in a hard-fought All-Ireland senior camogie championship final

(2) An emotional and exhausted Kilkenny manager Brian Dowling is congratulated by his wife Alison afterwards: "We've had a lot of hardship and bad luck in the group during the year and we said it ourselves, we're going to get that luck somewhere." That bad luck included cruciate injuries to sisters Aoife and Kellyann Doyle

(3) Captain Aoife Prendergast has the honour of lifting the O'Duffy Cup, a player who "epitomises everything about this group" according to manager Brian Dowling

(4) Cork's Fiona Keating, who contributed to an exciting final with 1-2, adopts a meditative pose on the Croke Park pitch. And so the curtain comes down early on a novel intercounty season

GALLERY OF FANS

AWARD WINNING IMAGES

sportsfile

OFFICIAL GAA PHOTOGRAPHERS

1997	1998	1999	2000	2001	2002
2003	2004	2005	2006	2007	2008
2009	2010	2011	2012	2013	2014
2015	2016	2017	2018	2019	2020

2021

Relive all the agony and ecstasy of past campaigns

A limited number of back issues of *A Season of Sundays* are available for €29.95 each, including post and packaging. To complete your set please send remittance, indicating the book(s) required, together with your name and address to:

Sportsfile, Patterson House, 14 South Circular Road, Portobello, Dublin 8, Ireland D08 T3FK

Alternatively shop online at: **www.sportsfile.com**

2022